NEW EARS

Thanks to Janet Ashworth, Kathie King, Mary Moore, the staff at FACES, and the rest of the folks at Syracuse University that contributed production support. Additional thanks to Armstrong Music for production assistance. Special thanks to my family and friends for their love and encouragement. New Ears is dedicated to those striving for excellence in creative careers.

NEW EARS
A GUIDE TO EDUCATION IN AUDIO AND THE RECORDING SCIENCES

Compiled & Edited
by
Mark Drews

The goal of New Ears is to present information about audio related programs and resources. No endorsement of included programs or resources is intended or implied. The information contained within was compiled from questionnaires and other reference materials. Its accuracy is based on the accuracy of the original resources. If any errors are contained within or if any notable program or resource was not included in this first edition of New Ears, please contact Mark Drews at New Ear Productions, 1033 Euclid Avenue, Syracuse, New York 13210. All comments are welcomed.

New Ears was produced using Ready, Set, Go™ 4.0 software on an Apple Macintosh II™ computer. Pages were produced on a NEC 890 Silentwriter™.

Preface

Just over ten years ago, I was a high school senior in search of an education that would allow me to become a music recording engineer. Music recording engineering? For some reason, this heading was not to be found in my search through college guides and other resources listing available fields of study. There were the traditional programs in music, electrical engineering, and perhaps acoustics, but all were separate degree programs and none combined elements of each into the multidisciplinary program that I desired. At the time, I felt the system could be improved somehow to provide more information about audio engineering programs to interested, prospective students. Luckily, I was able to find a program buried in the barrage of recruiting information that had been sent to me by various universities and was fortunate to receive a solid education in music and recording.

Since completing school six years ago, I have been overwhelmed by the number of calls and visits from students who were finding themselves in the same position that I had been in a decade earlier. Surely, my wish for a highly visable, comprehensive guide to audio and recording engineering schools had been fulfilled by a major publisher or industry organization, but apparently this was not the case. For every student I talked to, I was certain there had to be hundreds more that were experiencing unfruitful searches.

New Ears is an attempt to assist those students who are currently searching for information about education in audio and related areas. My desire to contribute to the future of audio education, along with the marvel of desktop publishing, have finally made this guide a reality. I invite the talented, the creative, the dedicated, and the determined to accept the academic challenges that will help prepare them for a career in the professional audio and recording industry. Best of luck.

Mark Drews
June 1989

237274

Using New Ears

New Ears consists of the following:

Introduction- These helpful hints will get you started.

New Ears' Potpourri- The Potpourri is provided for miscellaneous information aimed at interested readers.

Audio Publishers/Dealers- Providing names and addresses of several sources for obtaining books, video tapes, and computer software for audio, music, electronics, acoustics, video, film, and other audio related areas, this index also provides a list of ten classic audio texts for the new student.

Professional Industry Associations- This list includes over 25 audio, recording, music, and other related professional associations.

Magazines and Journals- Over 50 periodicals are indexed by category, including audiophile, audio recording, broadcast/video, consumer audio, electronic music, instrumental performance, manufacturer, music trades, and popular music magazines.

Profiled Programs- The heart of New Ears is a detailed listing of complete information on 70 audio and audio related programs. The programs are listed alphabetically by school name.

Additional Programs- This section contains basic information on several other programs not yet profiled.

Master List of Programs- Containing over 300 entries, the Master List includes schools from around the world that offer audio related programs. Programs are listed alphabetically by state or country.

Contents

Additional Schools/Programs 165

Master List of Schools/Programs Worldwide 181

Bibliography 207

Introduction

Welcome to New Ears. This guide is designed to assist you in finding educational opportunities in audio related fields and to act as a resource of additional audio and recording industry information. New Ears was assembled in response to the number of students that continue to be faced with the difficult task of finding a logical pathway to a career in audio. New Ears also provides useful information for other students, musicians, and working engineers interested in supplementing their knowledge of audio related areas by utilizing currently available magazines, books, seminars, short courses, trade schools, and university programs.

So you want to be an audio engineer...

The audio field is challenging, demanding, and diverse. It encompasses everything from sound recording and reinforcement to audio for television, radio, film, and more. The opportunities for careers are just as varied, from music engineering to audio equipment design to product sales and support. More importantly, the recent revolution in music and recording technologies has created positions that previously did not exist. Due to their diverse natures, most audio fields demand expertise in several disciplines, requiring the audio practitioner to have a command of the arts and the sciences. The individuals who successfully achieve this combination are unique, but these audio professionals often find themselves doing what they love, as opposed to doing what others might see as work.

Because the industry is forever changing and growing, it is always in need of bright, energetic, new minds to further the pursuit of creative and technical excellence in audio. The experience and education necessary to prepare yourself for an audio career is as challenging, demanding, and diverse as the industry itself. You will need to be well-educated, multi-talented, dedicated, and determined to successfully compete with your peers.

Getting a jump on an audio career...

If you are currently a high school student considering a career in audio, begin planning your education by utilizing resources that are immediately available to you. Use the following checklist as a guide:

Protect Your Ears. As obvious as this advice sounds, there are still too many people involved in audio that do not give enough thought to preserving this one irreplacible resource. Avoid extended exposure to high or constant sound pressure levels, including those experienced at loud concerts, factories, offices, and ironically enough, recording studios. Instrumentalists in large traditional orchestras, marching bands, and jazz/rock ensembles are also at risk of hearing loss from extended exposure while performing. Think of your ears as being equivalent to an athlete's legs; if you injure one or both, your active professional career is over.

Study Now. A strong background in computers, mathematics, music, and physics is essential for those considering a career in audio. Take advantage of college preparatory courses in these subjects offered by your high school. If your school also has courses in audio recording, electronic music, and radio/television broadcasting, you could be further ahead. You might also consider attending a summer audio workshop at one of the programs listed in New Ears.

Use Your Local Library. Take advantage of the wealth of magazines and books available to you that cover audio, music, and other areas of interest. Libraries can provide access to resources that you might not otherwise be in a position to obtain. In addition, most libraries have a system for requesting new book purchases and new magazine subscriptions. A hint for finding books on audio recording is to look in your library's card catalog or computer based reference system under the headings "audio", "music", and "sound recording". For more information, please refer to the Audio Publishers/Dealers index and the Magazines and Journals index.

Contact Professional Industry Associations. Several professional societies and associations are connected with the audio field. Those of primary interest to the audio student are the Acoustical Society of America (ASA), the Audio Engineering Society (AES), the National Academy of Recording Arts and Sciences (NARAS), the Society of Motion Picture and Television Engineers (SMPTE), the Society of Professional Audio Recording Services (SPARS), and the Recording Industry Association of America (RIAA). These are the fundamental governing bodies for the industry, and they offer a variety of support for audio and recording education. In particular, the AES offers annual scholarships for audio engineering students, and NARAS conducts an annual Grant/Research Opportunity Program for research in music recording and related areas. SPARS administers the National Studio Examination to provide audio students with a reference of their studio production knowledge. SPARS also provides internship and career counseling for students, as well as curriculum consultation for studio engineering schools. For addresses of these and other related societies and associations please refer to the New Ears' Professional Industry Associations Index.

Audio Program Categories

Seminars and Short Courses- Most short programs are intended to provide basic information on specific topics in a few hours or days. They are often used to refresh fundamentals or to introduce new technologies as part of a professional's continuing education.

Trade Schools- Trade school programs are often designed to train students in specific areas of the audio and recording industry, such as recording engineering or studio maintenance, over the course of several weeks or months.

University Programs- University offerings vary from individual courses through 2-year associate and minor degrees to extensive 4- and 5-year bachelor degrees. Opportunities for graduate studies are also available.

Selecting A Program

Seminars and short courses can provide you with basic exposure to the audio field and enhance your background if you are a working musician, engineer, or educator, but for the student seriously interested in an audio career, the selection of a program involves many personal decisions that go beyond simply choosing between a trade school or a university program. Regardless of which type of education you prefer, the following are advised:

Get as much information as possible on the programs that interest you. This includes writing or calling the schools for additional information not included in New Ears or school brochures. A phone call to a school is an efficient way of getting specific questions answered promptly.

Talk to local audio professionals and recent graduates about their educations. Former students can be excellent sources of information on the inner workings of various programs and the social aspects of the programs' respective schools.

Visit the schools of your choice. This gives you a chance to talk to faculty and current students, as well as an opportunity to tour the school and its facilities.

Apply early for admission to schools that have selective admissions requirements. This includes making sure that you have taken the necessary admissions tests (ACT, SAT), if required, and have filed any applicable scholarship or financial aid forms. This is very important if you are competing for a spot in a highly selective program. Informing admissions' personnel that you are **not** in need of any financial assistance can also be beneficial in some cases.

Select the best possible program that fits your personal preferences. There are countless other factors you must weigh when choosing a school, like costs, location, and size, but if you do your research properly, one or two programs should emerge from the pack that meet your personal requirements.

Once you're in...

Get Involved! This applies to your program and to the other aspects of your school's environment. The contacts you make within your program and the rest of the school's community can be as important as your formal education. Some of the greatest interdisciplinary success stories have resulted from school friends combining their talents during and after completing their educations. Your dormitory neighbor could become a film maker, a broadcast personality, a professional musician, or a banker one day, and benefit from your knowledge or vice versa.

Demand excellence from yourself. With the cost of education skyrocketing these days, you owe it to yourself, your parents, and whoever else is paying for your schooling to seriously apply yourself toward your educational goals. If you really want an eye opener, sit down and calculate the cost of your education per actual class period.

Demand excellence from your school. As with the above, your school should provide you with an education that fulfills or exceeds its promises and one that is cost effective, relative to the tuition charged. Education is, ideally, a mutually beneficial union between students, faculty, and knowledge.

Take the time needed to obtain a complete education. Do not feel a need to rush through school to get to your career. Proper education provides a strong, mature foundation upon which a professional career can then be built.

New Ears' Potpourri

Little Books of Big Interest

AES Directory of Educational Programs, $6 for non-members, prepared by the AES Education Committee, see industry index for address.

Annual Directory of Arts Internships,$25, California Institute of Arts, Office of Placement/Career Development, 24700 McBean Parkway, Valencia, CA 91355

APRS Guide to Recording in the UK, $6, compiled by Philip Vaughan, published by the APRS, see industry index for address.

NASM Directory of Music School Programs, $9, compiled by the NASM, see industry index for address.

NATTS' Handbook of Accredited Trade and Technical Schools, free, see industry index for address.

Non-profit Audio & Electronic Music Organizations

The Center for Electronic Music
432 Park Avenue South
New York, New York 10016
phone: 212-686-1755
CEM is profiled in New Ears.

Harvestworks, Inc.-Studio PASS
The Audio Arts Organization
596 Broadway (602)
New York, New York 10012
phone: 212-431-1130
Harvestworks/Studio PASS provides the art community with audio services, equipment access, and workshops in new technologies, They also offer MIDI programming & audio artist residencies for media artists.

Audio, Electronic Music, & Acoustics Research Centers

Center for Music & Technology
Case Western Reserve University
Department of Music, Haydn Hall
Cleveland, Ohio 44106

Center for Music Research
Florida State University
Tallahassee, Florida 32306

Acoustics & Vibrations Laboratory
Massachusetts Institute of Technology
Department of Mechanical Engineering
Building 3, Room 366
Cambridge, Massachusetts 02139

Center for Sound And Vibration
North Carolina State University
Campus Box 7910
Raleigh, North Carolina 27695

Computer Audio Research Laboratory
Center for Music and Related Research
University of California, San Diego
La Jolla, California 92093

Acoustics & Vibrations Laboratory
University of Hartford
College of Engineering
West Hartford, Connecticut 06117

Audio Research Group
University of Waterloo
Waterloo, Ontario
N2L 3G1 CANADA

Center for Computer Research in Music and Acoustics
Stanford University
Department of Music
Stanford, California 94305

Audio Publishers/Dealers

These publishers and book dealers are good sources of a wide variety of texts and references. Topic specializations are listed beneath their addresses. The Mix Bookshelf Catalog provides an overview of most titles available from the major audio publishers.

A-R Editions
315 West Gorham Street, Dept. 43
Madison, Wisconsin 53703
Digital audio, computer music books

Alan Gordon Enterprises, Inc.
Publications Department
1430 Cahuenga Boulevard
Hollywood, California 90078
Film, video books

Billboard Books
P.O. Box 2013
Lakewood, New Jersey 08701
Music industry books

Knowledge Industry Publications
701 Westchester Avenue
White Plains, New York 10604
Broadcast, video books

Mix Bookshelf Catalog
6400 Hollis Street, Suite 12
Emeryville, California 94608
Audio, video, electronics, music-books, videos, and software

Music Business Publications
P.O. Box 1191
Elmhurst, Illinois 60126
Music industry books

SAMS & Heyden Books
Howard W. Sam & Company
P.O. Box 7092
Indianapolis, Indiana 46207
Audio, electronics, video books, VIP Book Club

SIE Publishing
976 Fernhill Avenue
Newbury Park, California 91320
Audio recording books

Tab Books
Blue Ridge Summit, PA 17214
Audio, acoustics, electronics books

New Ears' List of Classic Audio Texts

How to Build a Small Budget Recording Studio From Scratch, by F. Alton Everest, TAB Books

Audio in Media, by Stanley Atlen, Wadsworth Publishing Company

The New Audio Cyclopedia, edited by Glenn Ballou, SAMS

The Handbook of Recording Engineering, by John Eargle, Van Norstrand Reinhold Company

Music, Physics, and Engineering, by Harry F. Olson, Dover Publications

Practical Techniques for the Recording Engineer, by Sherman Keane, SKE Publishing

Principles of Digital Audio, by Ken Pohlmann, SAMS

The Recording Studio Handbook, by John Woram, Sagamore Publishing Company

Sound Recording Practice, edited by John Borwick, Oxford University Press

Sound System Engineering, by Don and Carolyn Davis, SAMS

Professional Industry Associations

Academy of Motion Picture Arts and Sciences
8949 Wilshire Boulevard
Beverly Hills, California 90211
phone: 213-278-8990

Acoustical Society of America
American Institute of Physics
335 East 45th Street
New York, New York 10017
phone: 212-661-9404

American Cinema Editors
4426-1/2 Finley Avenue
Los Angeles, California 90027
phone: 213-660-4425

American Federation of Musicians
1501 Broadway, Suite 600
New York, New York 10036
phone: 212-869-1330

American Society of Composers, Authors, and Publishers
One Lincoln Plaza
New York, New York 10023
phone:213-466-8401

Association of AV Technicians
P.O. Box 603
Farmingdale, New York 11753

Association of Professional Recording Studios
163A High Street
Rickmansworth, Herts,
UNITED KINGDOM SD3 1AY
phone: 0923-772907

Audio Engineering Society
60 East 42nd Street
New York, New York 10165
phone: 212-661-8528

Broadcast Education Society
1771 North Street N.W.
Washington, DC 20036
phone: 202-429-5355

Broadcast Music Incorporated
320 West 57th Street
New York, New York 10019
phone: 212-586-2000

Canadian Recording Industry Assoc.
89 Bloor Street East
Toronto, Ontario
M4W 1A9 CANADA
phone: 416-967-7272

Computer Musicians Cooperative
3010 North Sterling Avenue
Peoria, Illinois 61604

IEEE Acoustics, Speech, & Signal Processing Society
445 Hoes Lane
P.O. Box 1331
Piscataway, New Jersey 08855

International MIDI Association
5316 West 57th Street
Los Angeles, California 90056
phone: 213-649-MIDI

MIDI Manufacturers Association
2265 Westwood Boulevard, #2223
Los Angeles, California 90064
phone: 213-649-MIDI

National Academy of Recording Arts and Sciences
303 North Glenoak Boulevard
Burbank, California 91505
phone: 818-843-8233

National Academy of Television Arts and Sciences
110 West 57th Street
New York, New York 10019
phone: 212-586-8424

National Association of Broadcasters
1771 North Street NW
Washington, DC 20036
phone: 202-293-3570

National Association of Jazz Educators
Box 724
Manhattan, Kansas 66502

National Association of Music Merchants
5140 Avenida Encinas
Carlsbad, California 92008
phone: 619-438-8001

National Association of Schools of Music
11250 Roger Bacon Drive, #21
Reston, Virginia 22090

National Association of Trade and Technical Schools
2251 Wisconsin Avenue NW
Washington, DC 20007

National Sound and Communications Association
501 West Algonquin Road
Arlington Heights, Illinois 60005
phone: 312-593-8360

Percussive Arts Society
214 West Main Street
Box 697
Urbana, Illinois 61801-0697

Recording Industry Association of America
1020 19th Street NW, Suite 200
Washington, DC 20036
phone: 202-775-0101

Society of Broadcast Engineers
7002 Graham Road, Suite 118
Indianapolis, Indiana 46220

Society of Motion Picture and Television Engineers
595 West Hartsdale Avenue
White Plains, New York 10607
phone: 914-761-1100

Society of Professional Audio Recording Services
4300 10th Avenue, North, Suite 2
Lake Worth, Florida 33461
phone: 407-641-6648

Many of these professional industry associations offer educational assistance and membership opportunities for students. The AES, NARAS, and NAMM also offer scholarships. A few offer their own guides to education, including the AES, NASM, and NATTS. MIX magazine also features audio education annually in their July issue. For those interested in the bottom line, Recording Engineer/Producer magazine has begun salary surveys of the industry featured annually. Pro Sound News is also a good source of dollars and cents information on salaries and the industry in general.

Magazines and Journals

Audiophile

The Absolute Sound
Box L
Sea Cliff, New York 11579
$33/year

The Audio Amateur
P.O. Box 576
Peterborough, New Hampshire 03458
$20/year

High Performance Review
P.O. Box 160010
Cupertino, California 95016
$20.97/year

IAR Hotline
P.O. Box 4271
Berkeley, California 94704
$28/year

The $ensible Sound
403 Darwin Drive
Snyder, New York 14226
$18/year

Audio Engineering

Acoustical Society of America Journal
American Institute of Physics
335 East 45th Street
New York, New York 10017
$380/year

Audio Engineering Society Journal
Audio Engineering Society
60 East 42nd Street
New York, New York 10165
$70/year for non-members

db
Sagamore Publishing Co., Inc.
203 Commack Road, Suite 1010
Commack, New York 11725
$15/year

Home & Studio Recording
Music Maker Publications, Inc.
22024 Lassen Street
Chatsworth, California 91311
$20/year

Home Recording
20085 Stevens Creek
Cupertino, California 95014
$15.95/year

IEEE-ASSP Journal
Box 1331
445 Hoes Lane
Piscataway, New Jersey 10017
$43/year

MIX
P.O. Box 3712
Escondido, California 92025
$24.95/year

Pro Sound News
2 Park Avenue
New York, New York 10016
$30/year, complimentary to industry

Studio Sound
Link House Magazines Ltd.
Link House, Dingwall Avenue
Croydon, CR9 2TA
United Kingdom
$52/year

Recording Engineer/Producer
Subscription Service
P.O. Box 12952
Overland Park, Kansas 66212
$24/year

Broadcast/Video

AV Video
25550 Hawthorne Boulevard
Suite 314
Torrance, California 90505
Complimentary to industry

Broadcast Management/Engineering
Subscription Department
P.O. Box 6056
Duluth, Minnesota 55806
Complimentary to industry

Broadcast Systems Engineering
Link House Magazines Ltd.
Link House, Dingwall Avenue
Croydon, CR9 2TA
United Kingdom
$40/year

International Broadcast Engineering
Marketing Dept., IBE, R.M. 206 S.H.
Queensway House
2 Queensway, Redhill
Surrey, United Kingdom
$80/year

Video Manager
Reader Service Department
P.O. Box 1002
Rye, New York 10580
Complimentary to industry

Videography
Media Horizons Inc.
50 West 23rd Street
New York, New York 10010
$25/year

Consumer Audio

Audio
P.O. Box 51011
Boulder, Colorado 80321
$19.94/year

High Fidelity
P.O. Box 10051
Des Moines, Iowa 50347
$11.97/year

Stereo Review
P.O.Box 52033
Boulder, Colorado 80321
$13.94/year

Electronic Music

Computer Music Journal
MIT Press Journals
55 Hayward Street
Cambridge, Massachusetts 02142
$28/year

Electronic Musician
Box 3747
Escondido, California 92025
$14.95/year

Keyboard Magazine
Subscription Department
20085 Stevens Creek
Cupertino, California 95014
$23.95/year

Music Technology
Music Maker Publications, Inc.
22024 Lassen Street
Chatsworth, California 91311
$25/year

Music, Computer, & Software
P.O. Box 625
Northport, New York 11768
$21/year

Instrumental Perfomance

Frets
Subscription Department
P.O. Box 4062
Cupertino, California 95015
$23.95/year

Guitar Player Magazine
Subscription Department
20085 Stevens Creek
Cupertino, California 95014
$23.95/year

Guitar Review
Albert Augustine Ltd.
40 West 25th Street
New York, New York 10010
$24/year

Keyboard Magazine
Subscription Department
20085 Stevens Creek
Cupertino, California 95014
$23.95/year

Modern Drummer
Modern Drummer Publications
P.O. Box 469
Cedar Grove, New Jersey 07009
$24.95/year

Musician
Subscription Department
P.O. Box 1923
Marion, Ohio 43306
$17/year

Percussion Notes
Percussive Arts Society
214 West Main Street
Box 697
Urbana, Illinois 61801
$20/year

Rhythm
Music Maker Publications
22024 Lassen Street
Chatsworth, California 91311
$17.70/year

The Strad
Novello & Company, Ltd.
Borough Green, Sevenoaks
Kent TN15 8DT
United Kingdom
$50/year

Windplayer
P.O. Box 7300
Van Nuys, California 91409
$12.95/year

Manufacturer
All manufacturer magazines are free.

Aftertouch
Yamaha Music Corporation
P.O. Box 7938
Northridge, California 91327

Banana News
Bananas at Large
802 Fourth Street
San Rafael, California 94901

Emuletter
E-mu Systems, Inc.
1600 Green Hills Road
Scotts Valley, California 95066
Complimentary to E-mu users

First Reflection
Alesis Corporation
3630 Holdrege Avenue
Los Angeles, California 90016

In Sync
New England Digital Corporation
Box 546
White River Junction, Vermont 05001

Roland Users' Group Magazine
Roland Corporation
7200 Dominion Circle
Los Angeles, California 90040

Tascam Playback
New Media Publications
145 Natoma Street
San Francisco, California 94105

Yamaha Academic News
Yamaha Music Corporation USA
30 Vreeland Road, Building A
Florham Park, New Jersey
Complimentary

Music Trades

Billboard
Billboard Publications
One Astor Plaza
1515 Broadway
New York, New York 10036
$178/year

Cashbox
330 West 58th Street
New York, New York 10019
$125/year

Grammy Pulse
NARAS
Suite 140 Mez.
303 North Glenoaks Boulevard
Burbank, California 91502
Complimentary to NARAS members

Up Beat
Maher Publications
180 West Park Avenue
Elmhurst, Illinois 60126
$15/year

Variety
Variety Inc.
475 Park Avenue South
New York, New York 10016
$100/year

Popular Music

College Musician
Alan Weston Communications, Inc.
303 North Glenoaks Blvd.,Suite 600
Burbank, California
$5.95/year

Down Beat
Maher Publications
180 West Park Avenue
Elmhurst, Illinois 60126
$18/year

Stage & Studio
25 Willowdale Avenue
Port Washington, New York 11050
$22/year

Musician
Subscription Department
P.O. Box 1923
Marion, Ohio 43306
$17/year

Pulse!
MTS, Inc.
Building C
2500 Del Monte Street
West Sacramento, California 95691
$19.95/year

Rolling Stone
Straight Arrow Publications
745 Fifth Avenue
New York, New York 10151
$15.95/year

Key to School Information and Abbreviations

The information in the New Ears' Listing of Audio Programs and Additional Programs is structured to provide the reader with a framework for comparing schools, based on fundamental data provided by participating programs. Please note that some information, such as **Program Length** and **Program Cost**, are given in varying relationship to each other. Some programs list the total cost of the program, while others list the cost per class, week, month, semester, or year. Under the categories labeled **Additional Resources** and **Classes Offered** a checkmark indicates the resources and classes available. **Profiles** are based on materials provided by the programs.

Abbreviations used for **Programs Offered** include:
> **A.A.-** Associate of Arts
> **A.A.S.-** Associate of Applied Sciences
> **A.S.-** Associate of Science
> **B.A.-** Bachelor of Arts
> **B.M.-** Bachelor of Music
> **B.S.-** Bachelor of Science
> **M.F.A.-** Master of Fine Arts
> **M.M.-** Master of Music
> **M.S.-** Master of Science
> **D.M.A.-** Doctor of Musical Arts

Common abbreviations used under **Accreditation** include:
> **N.A.S.M.-** National Association of Schools of Music
> **N.A.T.T.S.-** National Association of Trade and Technical Schools

Various regional associations of schools and colleges are also listed as accrediting agencies.

Abbreviations used under **Admission Prerequisites** include:
> **A.C.T.-** American College Test
> **G.E.D.-** General Equivalence Diploma
> **S.A.T.-** Scholastic Appitude Test

Any categories left blank indicate unsupplied information.

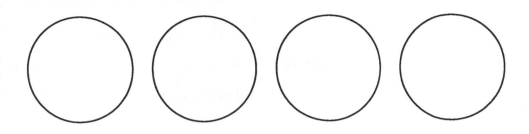

The New Ears' Listing
of
Audio Programs

Profiled Programs*
Additional Programs*
Master List**

Listed alphabetically by school name
**Listed alphabetically by state or country*

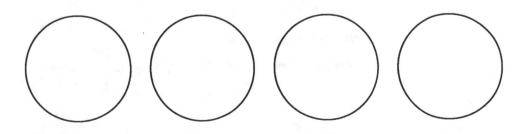

School:	*The Art Institute of Dallas*
Address:	*Two NorthPark*
	8080 Park Lane
	Dallas, TX 75231
Phone:	*800-692-8086*
Program Director:	*Terry Pope*
Admissions Director:	*Lee Colker*
Programs Offered:	*Music and Video Business*
Program Length:	*18 months*
Program Cost:	*$5,850 per academic year*
Program Established:	*1987*
Accreditation:	*NATTS*
Number of Studios:	*variable*
Tracks per Studio:	*8, 16, 24*
Types of Recording:	*Analog, Digital, Video*
Average Class Size:	*25 lecture, 8-12 lab*
Main Emphasis of Program:	*Professionalism, technique, production, and business*

Additional Resources:
Financial Aid √
Scholarships √
Professional Internships
Job Placement √

Admission Policy:	*Open*
Admission Prerequisites:	*High school diploma or GED certificate, personal or telephone interview with admissions representative*

Classes Offered:

Analog Electronics	√	Digital Electronics	√
Physics	√	Acoustics	√
Music Theory	√	Music Performance	
Microphone Techniques	√	Pure Stereo Techniques	√
Equipment Maintenance	√	Equipment Alignment	√
Video Techniques	√	Film Techniques	√
Business/ Marketing	√	Legal Aspects of Recording	√
Electronic Music Synthesis		Computer/ MIDI Techniques	√
Sound Reinforcement	√	Audio System Design	√

Profile:

The Art Institute of Dallas prepares its graduates for employment within the specific career areas of commercial art, interior design, fashion merchandising, and music and video business. The Institute's primary aim is to provide students with practical, employment related skills, and the curriculum is periodically modified to meet the needs of the local and national marketplace.

The Music and Video Business graduate is prepared for careers in both the business and technical aspects of the audio/visual fields. Courses include training in the areas of audio/visual promotion, production, and syndication; the use of studio recording and sound equipment; music and video business marketing and management; as well as legal areas such as contracts and copyrights.

In addition to concentrating on the development of each student's technical skills, the Institute places emphasis on personal and professional development to enhance the student's stature and growth.

School:	*Audio Recording Technology Institute*
Address:	*756 Main Street* *Farmingdale, NY 11735*
Phone:	*516-454-8999*
Program Director:	*Jim Bernard*
Admissions Director:	*Jim Bernard*
Programs Offered:	*Theory and Practice of Audio Recording*
Program Length:	*10 weeks per program*
Program Cost:	
Program Established:	*1973*
Accreditation:	*New York State*
Number of Studios:	*3*
Tracks per Studio:	*8*
Types of Recording:	*Analog*
Average Class Size:	*10*
Main Emphasis of Program:	*Hands-on studio training*
Additional Resources:	
Financial Aid	√
Scholarships	
Professional Internships	√
Job Placement	√
Admission Policy:	*Highly selective*
Admission Prerequisites:	*High school diploma, interview with director*

Classes Offered:

Analog Electronics	√	Digital Electronics	√
Physics	√	Acoustics	√
Music Theory		Music Performance	
Microphone Techniques	√	Pure Stereo Techniques	√
Equipment Maintenance	√	Equipment Alignment	√
Video Techniques		Film Techniques	
Business/ Marketing		Legal Aspects of Recording	
Electronic Music Synthesis		Computer/ MIDI Techniques	
Sound Reinforcement	√	Audio System Design	

Profile:

The Audio Recording Technology Institute offers three 10 week programs in recording engineering. The Basic Level program meets twice weekly and covers the fundamentals of audio engineering. Class lectures, group discussions, and question and answer periods systematically prepare students for their first recording session with a professional band, in the ninth week of the program.

Students continuing on with the Advanced Level program meet once a week for three hours and are exposed to acoustics, microphone technique, and console and tape recorder procedures in greater detail. Students are able to participate in a professional recording session, again, in their ninth week of study.

The final program offered is the Recording Workshop. Students meet once a week for a three hour recording session and experience how to deal with musicians as clients and how to maintain control of sessions as professional recording engineers. The program culminates with students completing a two hour mix individually and meeting with the director of the program to demonstrate their skills. Successful students can qualify to become freelance engineers at the studio and record their own sessions on a commission basis.

School:	*Bailie School of Broadcast*
Address:	*33 New Montgomery*
	San Francisco, CA 94115
Phone:	*415-541-0707*
Program Director:	*Adly Swanson*
Admissions Director:	*R. Bailie*
Programs Offered:	*Broadcasting, Video Production*
Program Length:	*9 months, 6 months*
Program Cost:	*$7,490 per program*
Program Established:	*1963*
Accreditation:	*NATTS*
Number of Studios:	*6*
Tracks per Studio:	*2*
Types of Recording:	*Analog, Digital, Video*
Average Class Size:	*12*
Main Emphasis of Program:	*Broadcasting- performance*
	Video- operations
Additional Resources:	
Financial Aid	√
Scholarships	
Professional Internships	√
Job Placement	√
Admission Policy:	*Selective*
Admission Prerequisites:	*High school diploma or GED certificate,*
	color perception-evaluation exam

Classes Offered:

Analog Electronics	Digital Electronics
Physics	Acoustics
Music Theory	Music Performance
Microphone Techniques	Pure Stereo Techniques
Equipment Maintenance	Equipment Alignment
Video Techniques √	Film Techniques
Business/ Marketing √	Legal Aspects of Recording
Electronic Music Synthesis	Computer/ MIDI Techniques
Sound Reinforcement √	Audio System Design

Profile:

The Bailie School's Broadcasting program offers students a chance to learn radio broadcasting with a hands-on approach. A variety of music formats are studied and taped. A thorough background in all aspects of the radio industry is part of the course of study.

Students in the Video Production course learn studio and field techniques in shooting, lighting, audio, writing and editing for video.

All instructors are actively employed in the radio/television field.

School:	*Ball State University*
Address:	*The Sound House- Music Annex 1*
	Ball State University
	Muncie, IN 47306
Phone:	*317-285-5537*
Program Director:	*Cleve Scott*
Admissions Director:	*Cleve Scott*
Programs Offered:	*Bachelor of Music-Music Engineering Technology*
Program Length:	*4 years*
Program Cost:	*$1,876 per year*
Program Established:	*1983*
Accreditation:	*NASM*
Number of Studios:	*5*
Tracks per Studio:	*2, 4, 8*
Types of Recording:	*Analog, Digital*
Average Class Size:	*12-20*
Main Emphasis of Program:	*Music engineering technology*

Additional Resources:
Financial Aid	√
Scholarships	√
Professional Internships	
Job Placement	

Admission Policy:	*Selective*
Admission Prerequisites:	*High school diploma, college preparation math, science, and music*

Classes Offered:

Analog Electronics	√	Digital Electronics	√
Physics	√	Acoustics	√
Music Theory	√	Music Performance	√
Microphone Techniques	√	Pure Stereo Techniques	√
Equipment Maintenance	√	Equipment Alignment	√
Video Techniques		Film Techniques	
Business/ Marketing		Legal Aspects of Recording	
Electronic Music Synthesis	√	Computer/ MIDI Techniques	√
Sound Reinforcement	√	Audio System Design	√

Profile:

The bachelor of music in Music Engineering Technology is one of the newest programs in the School of Music at Ball State University. It combines preparation in music composition, music performance, and music technology with a minor in applied physics (electronics). The MET curriculum is a uniquely designed to meet the expected standards of musical competence and incorporates basic proficiencies in science and technology. This interdisciplinary approach assures a graduate an excellent background for careers in areas where music is the primary product while science and technology are required for the media process. The MET program emphasizes music composition, sound synthesis, recording technology, computer applications, and telecommunication aspects of music distribution.

The course work requires people of dedication and excellence. Students are expected to attain junior standing as a performer, senior standing as a composer and the accomplishment of the applied physics minor. In addition, students are assigned individual projects in recording, equipment design, software development, and systems engineering.

The music curriculum includes concentration on individual performance, contemporary composition, commercial arranging, mixing and sound reinforcement. The physics requirements include mechanics, heat, light, sound and electronic theory in both audio applications and pulse and digital circuits. Students in the MET program are eligible, through competition, for employment as first and second engineers with Central Recording Services, University Singers, and the MET Studios.

This program is for the above average student who is disciplined and self-directed. It is for the energetic and the industrious. It requires long hours of hard work and a complete dedication to the goal of excellence in music.

School:	***Berklee College of Music***
Address:	*1140 Boylston Street*
	Boston, MA 02215
Phone:	*617-266-1400*
Program Director:	*David Moulton*
Admissions Director:	*Steve Lipman*
Programs Offered:	*Degree and Diploma Programs*
Program Length:	*4-5 years*
Program Cost:	*$6,390 plus lab fees per year for degree programs*
Program Established:	*1983*
Accreditation:	*NEASC*
Number of Studios:	*6, plus digital editing suite*
Tracks per Studio:	*Three-8, two-24, one-8 and 24*
Types of Recording:	*Analog, Digital, Video*
Average Class Size:	*<20 lecture, 8-12 lab*
Main Emphasis of Program:	*Professional skills in production,recording, and the general music industry*
Additional Resources:	
Financial Aid	√
Scholarships	√
Professional Internships	√
Job Placement	√
Admission Policy:	*Selective*
Admission Prerequisites:	*High school diploma, music background*

Classes Offered:

Analog Electronics		Digital Electronics	√
Physics	√	Acoustics	√
Music Theory	√	Music Performance	√
Microphone Techniques	√	Pure Stereo Techniques	√
Equipment Maintenance	√	Equipment Alignment	√
Video Techniques	√	Film Techniques	√
Business/ Marketing	√	Legal Aspects of Recording	√
Electronic Music Synthesis	√	Computer/ MIDI Techniques	√
Sound Reinforcement	√	Audio System Design	√

Profile:

Berklee College of Music offers Music Production and Engineering as a major course of study. Emphasizing both production and engineering skills, the major is a unique blend of artistic, technical and business studies. The program has been awarded MIX magazine's TEC Award (for Technical Excellence and Creativity) three times.

Classes are small and personal. Hands-on production and engineering projects are central to the curriculum, and students spend many hours in Berklee's six-studio complex. The faculty are all working professionals, including a studio owner, a video producer, several record producers, and a number of Boston's leading recording engineers. In addition, the program has very close ties to Berklee's new innovative Music Synthesis program and newly revamped Film Scoring program.

The Music Production and Engineering Program has approximately 275 majors enrolled. Berklee College of Music, with an enrollment of slightly less than 3,000 music students, is the ;largest College of Music in the world. Quincy Jones, Arif Mardin, Wynton Marsalls and Alan Silvestri are a few of Berklee's distinguished alumni.

Situated in Boston's Back Bay, Berklee is a central fixture in the rich and diverse musical and educational world of Boston, considered by many to be the finest center of higher education and culture in the world.

School:	*Blue Bear School of Music*
Address:	*Fort Mason Center- Bldg. D*
	San Francisco, CA 94123
Phone:	*415-673-3600*
Program Director:	*Steve Savage*
Admissions Director:	*Dennis Criteser*
Programs Offered:	*Home Recording, MIDI Studio Basics*
Program Length:	*5-8 weeks*
Program Cost:	*$100-$125*
Program Established:	*1981*
Accreditation:	*none*
Number of Studios:	*1*
Tracks per Studio:	*4, 16, MIDI studio*
Types of Recording:	*Analog, Sequencing*
Average Class Size:	*3 - 6*
Main Emphasis of Program:	*Home recording*

Additional Resources:
Financial Aid
Scholarships √
Professional Internships
Job Placement

Admission Policy:	*Open*
Admission Prerequisites:	*None*

Classes Offered:

Analog Electronics	Digital Electronics
Physics	Acoustics
Music Theory √	Music Performance √
Microphone Techniques	Pure Stereo Techniques
Equipment Maintenance	Equipment Alignment
Video Techniques	Film Techniques
Business/ Marketing	Legal Aspects of Recording
Electronic Music Synthesis √	Computer/ MIDI Techniques √
Sound Reinforcement	Audio System Design

Profile:

Blue Bear is primarily a music school. The current curriculum includes private lessons on most instruments and voice; group theory, singing and instrument classes; and playing workshops in popular music styles. Blue Bear also offers classes and seminars in music technology oriented to musicians and the home studio environment.

In addition to their Home Recording and MIDI Studio Basics classes, Blue Bear also periodically offers seminars on such topics as how to buy a synthesizer, MIDI sequencers, music electronics and acoustics, and drum machine programming. Private consultations are also available to address specific equipment setups and problems.

Blue Bear's special strength is addressing the technical needs of musicians, as distinct from engineers.

School:	*California Institute of the Arts*
Address:	*School of Music* *24700 McBean Parkway* *Valencia, California 91355*
Phone:	*805-255-1050*
Program Director:	*Alan Chaplin, Dean*
Admissions Director:	*Ken Young*
Programs Offered:	*B.F.A. in Music, specializing in Composition or Music Technology*
Program Length:	*4 years*
Program Cost:	*approx. $9,500 per year*
Program Established:	*1971*
Accreditation:	*NASM*
Number of Studios:	*4*
Tracks per Studio:	*Three 8 track, One direct to hard disk/ digital*
Types of Recording:	*Analog, Digital, MIDI*
Average Class Size:	*5-10*
Main Emphasis of Program:	*Contemporary music, including electronic, computer, and instrumental*
Additional Resources:	
Financial Aid	√
Scholarships	√
Professional Internships	√
Job Placement	√
Admission Policy:	*Selective*
Admission Prerequisites:	*Depends on program- scores or tapes for composers and audition for performers*

Classes Offered:

Analog Electronics	√	Digital Electronics	√
Physics	√	Acoustics	√
Music Theory	√	Music Performance	√
Microphone Techniques	√	Pure Stereo Techniques	√
Equipment Maintenance	√	Equipment Alignment	√
Video Techniques	√	Film Techniques	√
Business/ Marketing		Legal Aspects of Recording	√
Electronic Music Synthesis	√	Computer/ MIDI Techniques	√
Sound Reinforcement	√	Audio System Design	√

Profile:

The California Institute of Arts' School of Music is a leading focus for contemporary music on the West Coast. Students interested in the technical aspects of music can design their own specialization within the Music School. The four state-of-the-art Macintosh MIDI studios are available for individual student use 7 days a week, 24 hours a day. Instruction is offered in beginning and advanced synthesis, composition, audio, acoustics, and computer technology, as well as a full range of music courses, both traditional and contemporary. In addition, students are offered opportunities to work with visual artists, dancers, filmmakers, video artists, performance artists, and others within the various Schools in the Institute.

School:	*California State University-Chico*
Address:	*Department of Music*
	California State University-Chico
	Chico, CA 95929-0805
Phone:	*916-895-5152*
Program Director:	*Dr. Raymond Barker/Daniel Craik*
Admissions Director:	*Dr. Raymond Barker*
Programs Offered:	*Bachelor of Arts in Music,*
	Minor in Recording Arts
Program Length:	*4 years*
Program Cost:	*$450 per semester*
Program Established:	*1987*
Accreditation:	*NASM*
Number of Studios:	*2*
Tracks per Studio:	*8, 24*
Types of Recording:	*Analog, Digital, Video*
Average Class Size:	*15*
Main Emphasis of Program:	*The integration of the art of music with the technology of recording*
Additional Resources:	
Financial Aid	√
Scholarships	√
Professional Internships	
Job Placement	
Admission Policy:	*Open*
Admission Prerequisites:	*Must qualify for regular admission to any of the California State Universities*

Classes Offered:

Analog Electronics	√	Digital Electronics	
Physics	√	Acoustics	√
Music Theory	√	Music Performance	√
Microphone Techniques	√	Pure Stereo Techniques	√
Equipment Maintenance	√	Equipment Alignment	√
Video Techniques		Film Techniques	
Business/ Marketing		Legal Aspects of Recording	
Electronic Music Synthesis	√	Computer/ MIDI Techniques	√
Sound Reinforcement	√	Audio System Design	√

Profile:

The Department of Music at California State University, Chico, offers two programs in Recording Arts: the Bachelor of Arts in Music with an Option in Recording Arts, and the Minor in Recording Arts. Coordinated with these programs is the construction of state-of-the-art recording facilities in the West wing of the Performing Arts Center. The new facilities, available Fall, 1988, include a 24 track control room, a performance studio, and an electronic music studio.

The Option in Recording Arts provides a curriculum for students who wish to seek employment in fields combining music and technology. A music major in the Recording Arts Option will take courses in music history, music theory, composition with electronic media, and audio recording, along with courses from other departments in electronics and the physics of sound. Completion of a B.A. in this program will offer a music major enhanced employment opportunities in technical areas in the recording industry and in music synthesis. Employment opportunities can be further improved by pairing the Option in Recording Arts with a minor in an area such as business, telecommunications, engineering, computer science, or electronics.

As a corollary to the Option, the Minor in Recording Arts will assist students in other departments and disciplines to become more employable. It provides courses in music fundamentals, music appreciation, composition with electronic media, audio recording, electronics and physics. The Minor in Recording Arts will appeal to students majoring in areas such as Telecommunications, Engineering, Computer Science, Industrial Technology, Business, Theatre Arts, Dance, Education and Physical Education.

The Music Department at the University, with performing groups as diverse as the Chico Symphony Orchestra and the Jazz Ensemble, chamber quartets, operas and musicals, offers an ideal hands-on training laboratory for students in recording arts. The Option in Recording Arts for music majors includes an internship which provides the opportunity to record the major on campus productions. The recording studio is linked directly to the university's National Public Radio affiliated station, KCHO-FM, with the capability of live broadcasts and helps foster working relationships among students, faculty, and technicians in the performing arts, telecommunications, audio, and instructional media.

School:	*Capital University*
Address:	*Conservatory of Music* *2199 E. Main* *Columbus, OH 43209*
Phone:	*614-236-6226/6234*
Program Director:	*Robert Breithaupt*
Admissions Director:	*Robert Breithaupt*
Programs Offered:	*Beginning Engineering & Production,* *Advanced Engineering & Production, Studio* *Maintenance*
Program Length:	*5 weeks, 1 week, 1 week*
Program Cost:	*$3,000*
Program Established:	*1980*
Accreditation:	*NASM*
Number of Studios:	*6*
Tracks per Studio:	*One-8, two-16, three-24*
Types of Recording:	*Analog, Digital*
Average Class Size:	*90*
Main Emphasis of Program:	*Audio recording*
Additional Resources:	
Financial Aid	√
Scholarships	√
Professional Internships	
Job Placement	√
Admission Policy:	*Selective*
Admission Prerequisites:	*High school diploma*

Classes Offered:

Analog Electronics		Digital Electronics	
Physics	√	Acoustics	√
Music Theory	√	Music Performance	√
Microphone Techniques	√	Pure Stereo Techniques	√
Equipment Maintenance	√	Equipment Alignment	√
Video Techniques		Film Techniques	√
Business/ Marketing	√	Legal Aspects of Recording	√
Electronic Music Synthesis	√	Computer/ MIDI Techniques	√
Sound Reinforcement	√	Audio System Design	√

Profile:

The Conservatory of Music at Capital University, in conjunction with The Recording Workshop of Chillicothe, Ohio, offers to its students three programs in recording engineering and music production. Please see The Recording Workshop's profile for more information.

School:	*Casper College*
Address:	*Music Department* *125 College Drive* *Casper, WY 82601*
Phone:	*307-268-2532*
Program Director:	*Terry Gunderson*
Admissions Director:	*Terry Gunderson*
Programs Offered:	*Associate of Arts in Music*
Program Length:	*2 years*
Program Cost:	*$273/semester Wyoming residents,* *$733/semester non-residents*
Program Established:	*1984*
Accreditation:	*NCAC, NASM*
Number of Studios:	*1*
Tracks per Studio:	*8*
Types of Recording:	*Analog, Video*
Average Class Size:	*10*
Main Emphasis of Program:	*Music*
Additional Resources:	
Financial Aid	√
Scholarships	√
Professional Internships	
Job Placement	
Admission Policy:	*Open*
Admission Prerequisites:	*High school diploma*

Classes Offered:

Analog Electronics		Digital Electronics	
Physics	√	Acoustics	
Music Theory	√	Music Performance	√
Microphone Techniques	√	Pure Stereo Techniques	
Equipment Maintenance		Equipment Alignment	
Video Techniques	√	Film Techniques	
Business/ Marketing	√	Legal Aspects of Recording	
Electronic Music Synthesis	√	Computer/ MIDI Techniques	√
Sound Reinforcement		Audio System Design	

Profile:

Casper College offers audio students extensive hands-on experience in their first two years of college, experience which is usually reserved for juniors and seniors at four-year institutions. Following an introductory course and a course in Mixdown, students may enroll in Independent Study, a course which allows them to design and implement audio projects of their own choosing.

Casper College maintains a low student-teacher ratio in all its classes, assuring students individual attention in both their classes and their career counselling. The college offers the Associate of Arts degree with a strong transfer program for those wishing to continue on towards a Bachelor's Degree. Students can design a two year program which would allow them to transfer into baccalaureate programs in many areas, such as audio engineering, music business, and jazz studies, as well as more traditional programs in performance, education, theory, or history.

The Casper College Music Department is one of the few two year schools to be accredited by the National Association of Schools of Music. This assures the student that the audio program is supported by a solid music program, with training available in performance, history, theory, and jazz studies.

Casper College's campus consists of 28 buildings on 175 acres located at the foot of Casper Mountain in central Wyoming. Deer are frequent visitors to the campus in the fall, as well as the occasional bear. opportunities for hiking, hunting, fishing, and skiing are plentiful throughout the region.

School:	*Center for Electronic Music*
Address:	*432 Park Avenue South*
	New York, New York 10016
Phone:	*212-686-1755*
Program Director:	*Howard Massey*
Admissions Director:	*Howard Massey*
Programs Offered:	*20 different workshops on all aspects of music technology and audio production*
Program Length:	*2-4 weeks, 1 night per week*
Program Cost:	*$50-200 per workshop*
Program Established:	*1986*
Accreditation:	*none*
Number of Studios:	*2*
Tracks per Studio:	*4, 8*
Types of Recording:	*Analog, Digital*
Average Class Size:	*5-10 students*
Main Emphasis of Program:	*Electronic music and MIDI technology*

Additional Resources:
Financial Aid
Scholarships
Professional Internships √
Job Placement √

Admission Policy:	*Open*
Admission Prerequisites:	*None are required for most workshops. Prior experience is recommended for some advanced workshops.*

Classes Offered:

Analog Electronics	Digital Electronics	
Physics	Acoustics	
Music Theory	Music Performance	√
Microphone Techniques √	Pure Stereo Techniques	√
Equipment Maintenance	Equipment Alignment	√
Video Techniques √	Film Techniques	√
Business/ Marketing	Legal Aspects of Recording	
Electronic Music Synthesis √	Computer/ MIDI Techniques	√
Sound Reinforcement	Audio System Design	√

Profile:

The Center for Electronic Music is a unique, non-profit organization dedicated to providing the general public with information about and access to the latest in the state of the art music, MIDI, and audio equipment. To this end, they offer a series of regularly scheduled workshops each month, with topics ranging from "Synthesizer Basics" to "Introduction to MIDI" all the way to "Advanced Studio Production Techniques" and "Computer-Assisted Film and Video Scoring.

CEM also offers private instruction and consultation services, as well as access to a wide range of current synthesizer, sampler, computer, audio, and MIDI equipment. Their software library, consisting of over 200 programs for six different computers, is among the largest in the world. CEM benefits from broad support from over 50 major music manufacturers, as well as public and private donations.

Because CEM is subsidized through public and private grant monies, all fees for services are extremely low. They also offer a well-equipped 8 track production studio, with extensive SMPTE synchronization capabilities, which is rented by the hour for individual projects.

CEM also offers a yearly Artist In Residence program under (which selected artists are sponsored to realize their projects, free of charge) as well as an Outreach to the Schools program and a pioneering Outreach to the Disabled program, which provides equipment and music therapy services, free of charge, to disabled individuals in their homes and in hospitals.

School:	*City College of San Francisco*
Address:	*50 Phelan Avenue*
	San Francisco, CA 94112
Phone:	*415-239-3525*
Program Director:	*Phil Brown*
Admissions Director:	*Phil Brown*
Programs Offered:	*Audio Production, Radio Station Operation, Television Production*
Program Length:	*2 years*
Program Cost:	*$5 per unit*
Program Established:	*1945*
Accreditation:	*California Community Colleges*
Number of Studios:	*5 Audio, 1 Television, 1 Video Editing*
Tracks per Studio:	*4*
Types of Recording:	*Analog, Video*
Average Class Size:	*20*
Main Emphasis of Program:	*Audio and video*

Additional Resources:
Financial Aid √
Scholarships
Professional Internships √
Job Placement

Admission Policy:	*Open*
Admission Prerequisites:	*18 years of age*

Classes Offered:

Analog Electronics		Digital Electronics	
Physics		Acoustics	
Music Theory		Music Performance	
Microphone Techniques	√	Pure Stereo Techniques	√
Equipment Maintenance		Equipment Alignment	
Video Techniques	√	Film Techniques	
Business/ Marketing		Legal Aspects of Recording	
Electronic Music Synthesis		Computer/ MIDI Techniques	
Sound Reinforcement		Audio System Design	

Profile:

The Broadcasting Department at City College of San Francisco offers a two year program in Broadcasting. There are three emphases that students can take classes in: audio production, television production or radio station management; or students may take classes in all three emphases.

Classes include: mass media, history of broadcasting, non-dramatic writing for radio and television, announcing, beginning audio production, advanced multitrack audio production, studio television production, field production, video tape editing and the operation of a campus radio station. In addition there are a variety of short (5-8 weeks) workshops offered each semester.

The Broadcasting Department at City College of San Francisco feels that the only way students can learn production is to have their hands on the equipment, and this is where they place the emphasis in all of their classes.

School:	*Columbia College of Chicago*
Address:	*600 S. Michigan*
	Chicago, IL 60605
Phone:	*312-663-1600 ext. 252*
Program Director:	*Douglas Jones*
Admissions Director:	*Douglas Jones*
Programs Offered:	*B.A. in Radio with Sound Engineering, Sound Engineering Certificate*
Program Length:	*B.A.: 3-4 years, Certificate: 34 credit hours*
Program Cost:	*$156 per credit*
Program Established:	*1985*
Accreditation:	*NCAC*
Number of Studios:	*variable*
Tracks per Studio:	*24*
Types of Recording:	*Analog, Digital, Film*
Average Class Size:	*18*
Main Emphasis of Program:	

Additional Resources:
Financial Aid	√
Scholarships	√
Professional Internships	√
Job Placement	√

Admission Policy:	*Open*
Admission Prerequisites:	*High school diploma*

Classes Offered:

Analog Electronics	√	Digital Electronics	
Physics	√	Acoustics	√
Music Theory	√	Music Performance	√
Microphone Techniques	√	Pure Stereo Techniques	√
Equipment Maintenance	√	Equipment Alignment	√
Video Techniques	√	Film Techniques	√
Business/ Marketing	√	Legal Aspects of Recording	√
Electronic Music Synthesis	√	Computer/ MIDI Techniques	√
Sound Reinforcement	√	Audio System Design	√

Profile:

The primary objectives of the Radio Department's curriculum at Columbia College Chicago are to educate specialists in the creative, technical, and managerial aspects of the radio field, and to impress upon students an appreciation of the social and cultural potential of radio.

The curriculum is divided into two channels of study which may be combined or taken as distinct areas of concentration. The Laboratory concentration emphasizes production-oriented skills such as programming, performing, writing and directing. The Administrative/Management concentration develops expertise in sales, promotion, research, and merchandising.

For those students interested in working in the music business as recording engineers, a prescribed course of study is offered, including classes in sound engineering, acoustics for microphones, and advanced acoustical design. Successful candidates will be awarded a diploma upon completion of this program. Radio majors can specialize in Sound Engineering by taking these courses in addition to the Radio core curriculum.

Students not only learn in classes taught by professionals but can acquire college credits and hands-on experience through internships at one of the many radio stations, advertising agencies, and research firms in the Chicago area.

School:	*Community College of the Finger Lakes*
Address:	Music Recording Studio
	Lincoln Hill
	Canandaigua, NY 14424
Phone:	716-394-3500
Program Director:	Frank Verget
Admissions Director:	John Meuser
Programs Offered:	Associate in Arts with Music Recording, Music, or Broadcasting Concentration
Program Length:	2 years
Program Cost:	$672 per semester
Program Established:	1979
Accreditation:	Middle States, NYS Dept. of Education
Number of Studios:	1
Tracks per Studio:	16
Types of Recording:	Analog, Digital
Average Class Size:	16
Main Emphasis of Program:	Terminal or transfer music recording curriculum
Additional Resources:	
Financial Aid	√
Scholarships	√
Professional Internships	√
Job Placement	
Admission Policy:	Open
Admission Prerequisites:	None, but applicants are encouraged to undertake studies in music, math, and physical science if they plan to transfer to a 4-year school.

Classes Offered:

Analog Electronics	√	Digital Electronics	√
Physics	√	Acoustics	√
Music Theory	√	Music Performance	√
Microphone Techniques	√	Pure Stereo Techniques	√
Equipment Maintenance	√	Equipment Alignment	√
Video Techniques	√	Film Techniques	√
Business/ Marketing	√	Legal Aspects of Recording	√
Electronic Music Synthesis		Computer/ MIDI Techniques	√
Sound Reinforcement	√	Audio System Design	

Profile:

The Concentration in Music Recording is designed for students who are interested in sound recording and related areas of the music business. Students who earn the Associate in Arts degree with this concentration may transfer to four year schools offering similar baccalaureate majors or may choose to enter immediately into a career in the music or recording industries.

Community College of the Finger Lakes is also the home of the Finger Lakes Performing Arts Center. Under the auspices of the Rochester Philharmonic Orchestra, major artists such as Bob Dylan, Eric Clapton, Barry Manilow, The Beach Boys, James Taylor, and John Denver have performed on campus in recent years.

School:	*The Conservatory of Recording Arts and Sciences*
Address:	*14447 N. 20th Street*
	Phoenix, Arizona 85022
Phone:	*602-493-9898*
Program Director:	*Jaqueline F. Vlcan*
Admissions Director:	*Mary Goodenow*
Programs Offered:	*Audio Recording & Production, Electronic Music & MIDI, Music Business, Maintenance*
Program Length:	*3-6 months*
Program Cost:	*$2,053-$3,650*
Program Established:	*1988*
Accreditation:	*Arizona Private Post-Secondary Board*
Number of Studios:	*3*
Tracks per Studio:	*4, 16, 24*
Types of Recording:	*Analog, Digital*
Average Class Size:	*6 - 8*
Main Emphasis of Program:	*Recording and production*

Additional Resources:
Financial Aid
Scholarships
Professional Internships √
Job Placement √

Admission Policy:	*Open*
Admission Prerequisites:	*18 years of age, high school diploma/GED, interview*

Classes Offered:

Analog Electronics	√	Digital Electronics	√
Physics		Acoustics	√
Music Theory		Music Performance	
Microphone Techniques	√	Pure Stereo Techniques	√
Equipment Maintenance	√	Equipment Alignment	√
Video Techniques		Film Techniques	
Business/ Marketing	√	Legal Aspects of Recording	√
Electronic Music Synthesis	√	Computer/ MIDI Techniques	√
Sound Reinforcement		Audio System Design	

Profile:

The Conservatory of Recording Arts and Sciences' purpose is to train professionals for the audio recording and music industries. Through extensive hands-on training and practice with current production techniques, students gain confidence and expertise to move forward with their career goals. The Conservatory recognizes the unique quality of these fields in that they combine elements of creativity and technical skills, and the school utilizes this philosophy in its teaching methods.

The Director of Education, Wayne Vlcan, is a Gold Album winning engineer who previously owned a major 24 track studio in New York City. Wayne currently writes, engineers, and produces musical projects as well as jingles and scores for television and film.

School:	*East Texas State University*
Address:	*Music Department*
	Commerce, TX 75428
Phone:	*214-886-5303*
Program Director:	*Ron Yates*
Admissions Director:	*Wanda Yates*
Programs Offered:	*Minor in Music-Recording Emphasis*
Program Length:	*1-2 years or 4 years for degree*
Program Cost:	*$450 per semester*
Program Established:	*1985*
Accreditation:	*NASM*
Number of Studios:	*2*
Tracks per Studio:	*8*
Types of Recording:	*Analog*
Average Class Size:	*14*
Main Emphasis of Program:	*Music recording for Radio/TV or Advertising Art students*
Additional Resources:	
Financial Aid	√
Scholarships	√
Professional Internships	√
Job Placement	√
Admission Policy:	*Selective*
Admission Prerequisites:	*High school diploma or GED, 18 years of age,admission to major field of study-Radio/TV or Advertising/Art recommended*

Classes Offered:

Analog Electronics	√	Digital Electronics	√
Physics	√	Acoustics	√
Music Theory	√	Music Performance	√
Microphone Techniques		Pure Stereo Techniques	
Equipment Maintenance		Equipment Alignment	
Video Techniques	√	Film Techniques	
Business/ Marketing	√	Legal Aspects of Recording	
Electronic Music Synthesis	√	Computer/ MIDI Techniques	√
Sound Reinforcement		Audio System Design	

Profile:

The Recording Program offered through the Music Department at East Texas State University is designed to take a student through the basic and intermediate stages of multitrack studio techniques. It is offered to any student who qualifies for admission to the University, but three specific groups are primary targets for the program: 1. Music Majors, 2. Media Students, as a minor, and 3. part-time students, as personal enrichment. Program participants often serve as musicians for class projects and gain experience from both sides of the booth.

East Texas State University is located in Commerce, Texas, 65 miles northeast of Dallas, a leading jingle and commercial music center with some 60 active studios.

School:	*Ecole Superieure de Realisation Audiovisuelle*
Address:	*135 Avenue Felix Faure*
	75015 Paris
	FRANCE
Phone:	*1-45.54.56.58*
Program Director:	*Robert Caplain*
Admissions Director:	*Robert Caplain*
Programs Offered:	*Sound Design, Sound Engineering, Audiovisual Directing*
Program Length:	*3 years*
Program Cost:	*23,000 f per year*
Program Established:	*1972*
Accreditation:	
Number of Studios:	*4*
Tracks per Studio:	*2, 8*
Types of Recording:	*Analog, Digital, Video, Film*
Average Class Size:	*16*
Main Emphasis of Program:	*Audio,video, film production*

Additional Resources:
Financial Aid
Scholarships
Professional Internships √
Job Placement √

Admission Policy:	*Highly selective*
Admission Prerequisites:	*Secondary school diploma or equivalent, admissions interview*

Classes Offered:

Analog Electronics		Digital Electronics	
Physics	√	Acoustics	√
Music Theory		Music Performance	
Microphone Techniques	√	Pure Stereo Techniques	√
Equipment Maintenance		Equipment Alignment	
Video Techniques	√	Film Techniques	√
Business/ Marketing	√	Legal Aspects of Recording	
Electronic Music Synthesis		Computer/ MIDI Techniques	
Sound Reinforcement	√	Audio System Design	√

Profile:

ESRA believes that for a student to become a competent audio/visual director they must combine the talents of a feature film director with those of a communications expert. The work is both creative and technical. To have high quality sound in film requires not only a strong knowledge of visual methods, but requires specific training in sound, including acoustics and architectural acoustics, musical illustration, cinema, and sound production. ESRA insists on the importance of practical work; each student participates in a team to produce 12 films during their studies. Students specifically interested in sound can specialize in their third year of study.

Sound Director Robert Caplain is also the author of "Les techniques de prise de son" (The Techniques of Sound Recording). ESRA's program are presented in French.

During the months of July and August, the ESRA Cote D'Azur in Nice organize a one month seminar on the cinema, designed for French and foreign students from other disciplines. This holiday study course consists of lectures and work in practical techniques, direction of professional video film, visits to museums and studios, and participation in shows. The participants are able to make use of the University's accommodations and facilities.

School:	*Elmhurst College*
Address:	*190 Prospect* *Elmhurst, IL 60126*
Phone:	*312-279-4100 ext. 357*
Program Director:	*Tim Hays*
Admissions Director:	*Douglas Beach*
Programs Offered:	*Bachelor of Science and Bachelor of Music in Music Business*
Program Length:	*4 years*
Program Cost:	*$2,600 per semester*
Program Established:	*1974*
Accreditation:	*NCAC, Associated Colleges of Illinois*
Number of Studios:	*1*
Tracks per Studio:	*16*
Types of Recording:	*Analog*
Average Class Size:	*14*
Main Emphasis of Program:	*Professional training in the music business*

Additional Resources:
Financial Aid √
Scholarships √
Professional Internships √
Job Placement

Admission Policy:	*Selective*
Admission Prerequisites:	*High school diploma, ACT or SAT scores, music audition*

Classes Offered:

Analog Electronics	√	Digital Electronics	
Physics	√	Acoustics	
Music Theory	√	Music Performance	√
Microphone Techniques	√	Pure Stereo Techniques	√
Equipment Maintenance		Equipment Alignment	
Video Techniques	√	Film Techniques	
Business/ Marketing	√	Legal Aspects of Recording	√
Electronic Music Synthesis	√	Computer/ MIDI Techniques	√
Sound Reinforcement		Audio System Design	

Profile:

Located in the Chicago metropolitan area, Elmhurst College is a nationally accredited institution that offers both a Bachelor of Science degree and a Bachelor of Music degree in Music Business. In addition to classwork in music, business and the business of music, students get hands-on industry experience through internships, industry speakers and course tours to locations as diverse as los Angeles, New York City and West Germany.

Resources include a new16 track studio in the College's new Computer and Technology Center, recently expanded practice and recital facilities and an artist faculty of over 30. Industry support is provided in the form of scholarships from organizations such as NAMM and NARAS, corporate sponsorship, a student chapter of the MEIEA and an intern/job bank.

Offering students individualized instruction in music business for over 17 years, Elmhurst provides a specialized career track integrated within a 4 year degree.

School:	*Evergreen State College*
Address:	*LIB 1326 TESC*
	Olympia, WA 98505
Phone:	*206-866-6000*
Program Director:	*Peter Randlette*
Admissions Director:	*Peter Randlette*
Programs Offered:	*Interdisciplinary Liberal Arts*
Program Length:	*variable*
Program Cost:	
Program Established:	
Accreditation:	
Number of Studios:	*5*
Tracks per Studio:	*4, 8, 16*
Types of Recording:	*Analog, Video, Film*
Average Class Size:	*10-14*
Main Emphasis of Program:	*Musical applications of multitrack recording techniques*
Additional Resources:	
Financial Aid	√
Scholarships	
Professional Internships	√
Job Placement	
Admission Policy:	*Selective*
Admission Prerequisites:	*High quality academic history*

Classes Offered:

Analog Electronics		Digital Electronics	
Physics		Acoustics	
Music Theory	√	Music Performance	√
Microphone Techniques	√	Pure Stereo Techniques	
Equipment Maintenance		Equipment Alignment	
Video Techniques	√	Film Techniques	√
Business/ Marketing	√	Legal Aspects of Recording	
Electronic Music Synthesis	√	Computer/ MIDI Techniques	√
Sound Reinforcement	√	Audio System Design	√

Profile:

Evergreen State College is an undergraduate liberal arts school with no departments, 101 type classes or grades. Students take programs which are full time and study a subject with many of its associated components. Students receive written evaluations of their work. In audio related areas, a student may be in a class like Experiments in Light and Sound. Members become proficient in audio and electronic music production skills, learn video production skills and study the history of composition with images and sound. Third and fourth year students may design their own learning contracts. Evergreen State College does not offer tradition recording institute style education, nor do we teach audio skills separate from their applications in music, audio production and film/video.

Evergreen State College students tend to have broader overviews on the production process, and often have special skills in addition to audio production. They have an excellent placement record within the industry.

School:	*Five Towns College*
Address:	*2165 Seaford Avenue* *Seaford, NY 11783*
Phone:	*516-783-8800*
Program Director:	*Joseph Carbone*
Admissions Director:	*Fred Gladstone*
Programs Offered:	*Audio Recording Technology, Video Arts*
Program Length:	*2 years*
Program Cost:	*$4,250 per year*
Program Established:	*1979*
Accreditation:	*Middle States Assoc., NYS Board of Regents*
Number of Studios:	*1*
Tracks per Studio:	*24*
Types of Recording:	*Analog, Video*
Average Class Size:	*15*
Main Emphasis of Program:	*Business management, audio, video*

Additional Resources:
Financial Aid √
Scholarships √
Professional Internships √
Job Placement √

Admission Policy: *Open*

Admission Prerequisites: *High school diploma or equivalent*

Classes Offered:

Analog Electronics	√	Digital Electronics	
Physics		Acoustics	√
Music Theory	√	Music Performance	√
Microphone Techniques	√	Pure Stereo Techniques	√
Equipment Maintenance	√	Equipment Alignment	√
Video Techniques	√	Film Techniques	√
Business/ Marketing	√	Legal Aspects of Recording	√
Electronic Music Synthesis	√	Computer/ MIDI Techniques	√
Sound Reinforcement	√	Audio System Design	√

Profile:

Five Towns College offers the A.A.S. degree program in Business Management with concentrations in Audio Recording Technology, Video Arts, Music Business, Jazz and Commercial Music, and others. The programs are intended for students who wish to enter the business world directly after completion of their college studies and consist of a business and liberal arts core in addition to the program of concentration.

The Audio Recording Technology concentration provides students with the knowledge, skills, and understanding required for them to enter the audio recording field. Courses cover everything from basic audio and acoustic theory, through multitrack recording, signal processing, equipment alignment, studio design, and automated mixdown, to business procedures for operating a professional studio. In addition, the school offers a concentration in Electronic Music Instrument Technology for learning the troubleshooting and repair of electronic musical instruments and related audio equipment, including recording gear.

The Video Arts concentration provides students with a knowledge of the equipment, materials, and processes used in video studios and teaches them the planning, scripting, directing, and editing skills required to create various types of video productions. Courses offered in the program include microphone and lighting techniques, special effects, lip-sync recording, multi-camera production, portable video formats, and production scheduling.

School:	*Full Sail Center for the Recording Arts*
Address:	*658 Douglas Avenue*
	Altamonte Springs, FL 32714
Phone:	*407-788-2450 or 800-221-2747*
Program Director:	*Garry Jones*
Admissions Director:	*Joan Daubresse*
Programs Offered:	*Recording Engineering, Synclavier & MIDI, Sound Reinforcement, and others*
Program Length:	*3-5 week courses, 10 month comprehensive program*
Program Cost:	*$720-1,980 per course, $11,390 comprehensive program*
Program Established:	*1978*
Accreditation:	*NATTS*
Number of Studios:	*1 plus a mobile unit*
Tracks per Studio:	*24 in PARC studio, 48 in mobile*
Types of Recording:	*Analog, Digital, Video*
Average Class Size:	*24*
Main Emphasis of Program:	*Recording engineering and producing*

Additional Resources:
Financial Aid √
Scholarships
Professional Internships √
Job Placement √

Admission Policy:	*Selective*
Admission Prerequisites:	*High school diploma, GED, or college diploma, physical and hearing exam, references*

Classes Offered:

Analog Electronics	√	Digital Electronics	√
Physics		Acoustics	√
Music Theory		Music Performance	
Microphone Techniques	√	Pure Stereo Techniques	√
Equipment Maintenance	√	Equipment Alignment	√
Video Techniques	√	Film Techniques	
Business/ Marketing		Legal Aspects of Recording	√
Electronic Music Synthesis	√	Computer/ MIDI Techniques	√
Sound Reinforcement	√	Audio System Design	√

Profile:

The creative learning opportunities offered at Full Sail include the following- Synclavier, MIDI Music, Music Business, Recording Engineering, Advanced Recording & Production, Studio Maintenance & Trouble Shooting, Sound Reinforcement & Remote Recording, and the Recording Arts Comprehensive Program. The focus of all courses is to provide in-studio, hands-on, practical experience in music recording and engineering, video production, and related areas of the music industry. Many diverse job opportunities are represented within these categories. The Full Sail student receives an introduction to each career field, including an overview of what each position requires, its Income potential, lifestyle, job security, and the demand for entry-level jobs. Students are taught by and hear first-hand experiences from current industry professionals. These instructors and guest lecturers share both successes and failures to prepare students for their chosen career. Additionally, students receive step-by-step guidance on how to enter the job market.

All courses are taught in Altamont Springs, Florida and feature up to 1320 hours of total instruction. Classrooms and hands-on studio labs are located at Full Sail headquarters, a complex housing administrative offices, classrooms, a 24 track state of the art recording studio featuring a Solid State Logic console, a 48 track mobile recording unit, and a studio facility for audiophile digital real-time cassette duplication. A portion of the specialized instruction is conducted in various audio, video, and film production facilities in the central Florida area.

Established by Jon Phelps in 1979, Full Sail grew from the need for a quality program taught by current industry professionals using up to date equipment.

School:	*Fullerton College*
Address:	*321 E. Chapman Avenue*
	Fullerton, CA 92634
Phone:	*714-992-7296*
Program Director:	*Alex Cima*
Admissions Director:	*Apply to College's Admissions Office*
Programs Offered:	*Music Recording/Production Certificate,*
	Commercial Music
Program Length:	*1-2 years*
Program Cost:	*$50/semester California residents*
Program Established:	*1981*
Accreditation:	*Western Association of Schools & Colleges,*
	California State Dept. of Education
Number of Studios:	*1 plus electronic music lab*
Tracks per Studio:	*24*
Types of Recording:	*Analog, Digital*
Average Class Size:	*10-45*
Main Emphasis of Program:	*Music recording/production*

Additional Resources:
Financial Aid   √
Scholarships   √
Professional Internships
Job Placement

Admission Policy:	*Open*
Admission Prerequisites:	*High school diploma or GED, open admission*
	for those over18, see college catalog for
	more information

Classes Offered:

Analog Electronics   Digital Electronics
Physics   Acoustics
Music Theory   √   Music Performance   √
Microphone Techniques   √   Pure Stereo Techniques
Equipment Maintenance   Equipment Alignment
Video Techniques   Film Techniques
Business/ Marketing   √   Legal Aspects of Recording √
Electronic Music Synthesis   √   Computer/ MIDI Techniques
Sound Reinforcement   Audio System Design

Profile:

The Recording/Production Certificate at Fullerton College is a music oriented, one year, full time program designed to train students in professional audio recording and music production techniques. A Certificate in Recording/Production includes two semesters of recording, two semesters of electronic music synthesis, one semester of music business, in addition to music theory, survey, and performance courses. Options include an Associate in Arts degree in Music and/or transfer programs that enable students to complete a Bachelor of Arts degree at a four year institution.

The Music Department at Fullerton College has a fully equipped, professional 24 track recording studio and electronic music lab. The program has achieved national recognition for excellence from several industry groups and publications, including a nomination in 1985 for MIX magazine's TEC award as one of the ten best recording programs in the United States.

School:	*The Grove School of Music*
Address:	*14539 Sylvan Avenue*
	Van Nuys, CA 91411
Phone:	*818-904-9400*
Program Director:	*Paul Goldfield*
Admissions Director:	*Mike Julian*
Programs Offered:	*Recording Engineer Program*
Program Length:	*1 year*
Program Cost:	*$5,675*
Program Established:	*1983*
Accreditation:	*NASM*
Number of Studios:	*3*
Tracks per Studio:	*8, 16, 24*
Types of Recording:	*Analog, Video*
Average Class Size:	*25*
Main Emphasis of Program:	*Audio engineering*

Additional Resources:
Financial Aid √
Scholarships √
Professional Internships √
Job Placement √

Admission Policy: *Selective*

Admission Prerequisites: *Interview with program director, completion of engineering program questionaire*

Classes Offered:

Analog Electronics	√	Digital Electronics	
Physics	√	Acoustics	√
Music Theory	√	Music Performance	√
Microphone Techniques	√	Pure Stereo Techniques	√
Equipment Maintenance	√	Equipment Alignment	√
Video Techniques	√	Film Techniques	√
Business/ Marketing	√	Legal Aspects of Recording	
Electronic Music Synthesis	√	Computer/ MIDI Techniques	√
Sound Reinforcement	√	Audio System Design	√

Profile:

The Grove School of Music offers intensive, one year programs designed to help students move quickly and confidently toward professional careers as performers, composers, producers, or audio/video engineers. The Recording Engineering Program consists of a minimum of 710 class hours studying recording engineering and general musicianship. Engineering courses Include: Music Acoustics and Physics, Recording Theory, Advanced 8 Track Techniques, Studio Management, Sound Reinforcement, Studio Maintenance, 24 Track Recording, Synthesis, Fundamentals of Electronics, and Recording Lab.

In the school's three recording studios, recording engineering students are given a wide range of opportunities to record and film all types of musical performances, from soloists to 45 piece orchestras. The school also has four electronic music synthesis labs that can be utilized by recording engineering students.

School:	*Horizon Recording Studio*
Address:	*1317 South 295 Place*
	Federal Way, WA 98003
Phone:	*206-941-2018*
Program Director:	*Bill Gibson*
Admissions Director:	*Roger Wood*
Programs Offered:	*Basic and Advanced Recording*
Program Length:	*6 weeks and 8 weeks*
Program Cost:	*$395-Basic, $495-Advanced*
Program Established:	*1979*
Accreditation:	
Number of Studios:	*1*
Tracks per Studio:	*24*
Types of Recording:	*Analog, Digital, Film*
Average Class Size:	*6*
Main Emphasis of Program:	*24-track recording techniques*
Additional Resources:	
Financial Aid	
Scholarships	
Professional Internships	
Job Placement	
Admission Policy:	*Open*
Admission Prerequisites:	*None*

Classes Offered:

Analog Electronics	√	Digital Electronics	√
Physics		Acoustics	√
Music Theory		Music Performance	
Microphone Techniques	√	Pure Stereo Techniques	
Equipment Maintenance	√	Equipment Alignment	√
Video Techniques		Film Techniques	
Business/ Marketing		Legal Aspects of Recording	
Electronic Music Synthesis		Computer/ MIDI Techniques	√
Sound Reinforcement		Audio System Design	√

Profile:

Horizon Recording Studios offers two programs in recording engineering: Basic and Advanced Multitrack Recording. The Basic program is intended for those students with little or no previous experience in recording. Emphasis is on basic recording principles and techniques as well as hands-on experience recording, overdubbing, and mixing live performances. The 30 hour program is taught on weekends over the course of six weeks. The textbook, study materials, and recording tape required for the program is included in its cost.

The Advanced Multitrack Recording program is offered to those who have completed the Basic program or for those who have the equivalent background experience. The program provides a continuation of basic principles and techniques and emphasizes conducting sessions and attaining special effects using signal processing gear. The 40 hour program is taught over the course of eight weeks.

Horizon is primarily a professional 24 track recording school and is not a vocational school. Classes are avocational and intended to give students a broad overview of recording principles and techniques. Classes are taught by experienced engineer/producers and give students and laboratory bands an opportunity to learn while participating in multitrack recording sessions.

School:	*Houston Community College*
Address:	*Commercial Music Department*
	901 Yorkchester
	Houston, TX 77079
Phone:	*713-468-6891*
Program Director:	*Aubrey Tucker*
Admissions Director:	*Mark Erickson*
Programs Offered:	*A.A.S. in Audio Recording Technology*
Program Length:	*2 years*
Program Cost:	*$1,600 Texas residents,*
	$4,000 non-residents
Program Established:	*1985*
Accreditation:	*SACS*
Number of Studios:	*2*
Tracks per Studio:	*16-24*
Types of Recording:	*Analog, Digital, Video, Film*
Average Class Size:	*15*
Main Emphasis of Program:	*Recording engineering education*

Additional Resources:
Financial Aid √
Scholarships √
Professional Internships √
Job Placement √

Admission Policy:	*Open*
Admission Prerequisites:	*High school diploma or GED*

Classes Offered:

Analog Electronics	√	Digital Electronics	√
Physics	√	Acoustics	√
Music Theory	√	Music Performance	√
Microphone Techniques	√	Pure Stereo Techniques	√
Equipment Maintenance	√	Equipment Alignment	√
Video Techniques	√	Film Techniques	√
Business/ Marketing	√	Legal Aspects of Recording	√
Electronic Music Synthesis	√	Computer/ MIDI Techniques	√
Sound Reinforcement	√	Audio System Design	√

Profile:

The Commercial Music Department at Houston Community College offers two year programs in Audio Engineering Technology, Performance, and Composition/Arranging/Copying that lead to Associate in Arts degrees. The programs are designed to provide students with the essential knowledge, skills, and experience to prepare them for employment in the contemporary music industry. Emphasizing country, rock, and jazz music, the graduate of the Commercial Music department is prepared to enter the industry as a performing musician, composer/arranger, merchant, and/or audio engineer.

Houston is gaining a reputation as a major production center for motion pictures, television, and the recording industry, and graduates of the Commercial Music curricula will have a wide variety of employment opportunities waiting for them in the local area.

School:	*Hutchinson Vocational Technical Institute*
Address:	*200 Century Avenue*
	Hutchinson, MN 55350

Phone:	*612-587-3636*
Program Director:	*David Igl*
Admissions Director:	*David Igl*
Programs Offered:	*Audio Visual Technology*

Program Length:	*18 months*
Program Cost:	*$1,285 per program*
Program Established:	*1973*
Accreditation:	*NCCS, Minnesota Department of Education*
Number of Studios:	*2*
Tracks per Studio:	*2, 8*
Types of Recording:	*Analog, Digital , Video*
Average Class Size:	*12*
Main Emphasis of Program:	*Audio and video engineering*

Additional Resources:

Financial Aid	√
Scholarships	√
Professional Internships	√
Job Placement	√

Admission Policy:	*Open*
Admission Prerequisites:	*High school diploma or equivalent*

Classes Offered:

Analog Electronics	√	Digital Electronics	√
Physics		Acoustics	√
Music Theory		Music Performance	
Microphone Techniques	√	Pure Stereo Techniques	√
Equipment Maintenance	√	Equipment Alignment	√
Video Techniques	√	Film Techniques	
Business/ Marketing	√	Legal Aspects of Recording	√
Electronic Music Synthesis		Computer/ MIDI Techniques	√
Sound Reinforcement	√	Audio System Design	√

Profile:

The Audio/Video Technology program at the Technical Institute of Hutchinson offers students the choice of concentration of studies and accompanying diploma in either audio or video technology. One of the most unique aspects of the Institute is its personalized instruction systems which allows students to start their training on any Monday, to get credit for previous experience, and to proceed through their training at an accelerated pace. This allows the more mature student the opportunity to retrain for new careers or to upgrade their skills more conveniently than many traditional college course delivery systems.

The Audio Technology program of instruction offers a challenging curriculum which is balanced between theory and operation of all types of audio equipment and the technical understanding of the analog and digital electronics used to make the equipment work. Students enrolling in this program should have a strong background in math, balanced with a well developed ear for music.

Career opportunities for graduates of the Audio program include sound reinforcement, including installation of public address systems, running sound for bands in nightclubs or working for sound reinforcement companies doing sound for conference, conventions, and concert tours. Graduates are also qualified for entry level employment in pro audio dealerships and studios doing recording, broadcast production, technical maintenance and repair. On the job, graduates install, operate, and perform routine maintenance on recorders, mixing consoles, amplifiers, speakers, electronic instruments and a variety of audio signal processing devices.

Students intending to begin a career in video production need proficiency in three areas: 1) Basic skills involved in equipment theory and operations, 2) Human relation skills, the ability to get along with co-workers, and 3) The skills and self-confidence necessary to work effectively in a pressure situation and solve technical problems. The video curriculum offers courses that allow students to master these skill areas. The curriculum is very project oriented and allows students to develop their ability to work on both self-directed projects and in group setting. Students entering the video program should display the characteristics of being warmly enthusiastic, imaginative and ingenious.

School:	*Indiana University*
Address:	*School of Music*
	Bloomington, IN 47405
Phone:	*812-335-1900*
Program Director:	*David Pickett*
Admissions Director:	*David Pickett*
Programs Offered:	*Associate of Science in Audio Technology*
Program Length:	*5 semesters*
Program Cost:	*$63/credit hour Indiana residents, $181/credit hour non-residents*
Program Established:	*1981*
Accreditation:	*NASM*
Number of Studios:	*3*
Tracks per Studio:	*2, 2, 16*
Types of Recording:	*Analog, Digital*
Average Class Size:	*10*
Main Emphasis of Program:	*Classical recording*

Additional Resources:
Financial Aid √
Scholarships √
Professional Internships √
Job Placement √

Admission Policy:	*Highly selective*
Admission Prerequisites:	*Indiana University admissions requirements, over-all academic and musical record, personal interview*

Classes Offered:

Analog Electronics	√	Digital Electronics	√
Physics	√	Acoustics	√
Music Theory	√	Music Performance	√
Microphone Techniques	√	Pure Stereo Techniques	√
Equipment Maintenance	√	Equipment Alignment	√
Video Techniques		Film Techniques	
Business/ Marketing		Legal Aspects of Recording	
Electronic Music Synthesis	√	Computer/ MIDI Techniques	
Sound Reinforcement	√	Audio System Design	√

Profile:

The strengths of the Indiana University Audio Program are based on its interaction with the Internationally acclaimed musical talent in the IU Music School. Apart from formal classes in electronics and audio theory and practice, students have ample opportunity to experiment with recording set-ups in a variety of different situation, all involving musical performances of the highest caliber.

Examples of this range on a weekly basis from fully-staged operas , symphony, and jazz concerts to daily student and faculty recitals. These take place in the Musical Arts Center and Recital Hall, both of which have fully equipped recording booths. Student made recordings have appeared on the NPR World of Opera, BBC Radio 3, and the Music from Indiana series.

The program stresses musical values and interaction with musicians. Practical experience is also given in recording sessions, from multitrack sessions of pop and commercial music through direct to digital stereo recordings involving all types of serious music. The school has recently published a CD of string quartets by Karl Weigl, Malipiero, and Turina as part of a new series of prestigious recordings.

School:	*Institute of Audio Research*
Address:	*64 University Place* *New York, NY 10003*
Phone:	*212-677-7580*
Program Director:	*Philip Stein*
Admissions Director:	*Philip Stein*
Programs Offered:	*Multitrack Recording Technology* *Video Technology Program*
Program Length:	*MRT-9 months, VTP-1 year*
Program Cost:	*MRT-$5,988, VTP-$6,488*
Program Established:	*1969*
Accreditation:	*NYS Department of Education, NATTS*
Number of Studios:	*2*
Tracks per Studio:	*24, 36*
Types of Recording:	*Analog*
Average Class Size:	*18*
Main Emphasis of Program:	*MRT-Recording engineering* *VTP-Video maintenance and repair*
Additional Resources:	
Financial Aid	√
Scholarships	
Professional Internships	√
Job Placement	√
Admission Policy:	*Selective*
Admission Prerequisites:	*High school diploma or equivalent*

Classes Offered:

Analog Electronics	√	Digital Electronics	√
Physics	√	Acoustics	√
Music Theory	√	Music Performance	
Microphone Techniques	√	Pure Stereo Techniques	√
Equipment Maintenance	√	Equipment Alignment	√
Video Techniques	√	Film Techniques	
Business/ Marketing		Legal Aspects of Recording	
Electronic Music Synthesis	√	Computer/ MIDI Techniques	√
Sound Reinforcement	√	Audio System Design	√

Profile:

The Institute of Audio Research is a propriety technical training facility located in the heart of historic Greenwich Village. The Institute trains entry level personnel for the professional music, audio, and video industries. The Institute offers Multitrack Recording Technology, Video Technology, and Audio & Video Electronics Technology programs, along with short courses and industrial training for specific applications.

The Multitrack Recording Technology program is offered with two options. The first option allows the student to take the entire 600 hour program in 9 months as a full time student or in 15 months as a part time student. The second option is designed for the student enrolled in a four year degree curriculum and allows them to complete the MRT program over the course of two summers. Both options provide up to 31 transfer credits toward several college bachelor degree programs.

The Video Technology program trains students for entry level technical positions in the maintenance, repair, and operations of professional video equipment. The program can be taken full time in one year or part time in 18 months. NYU offers 51 transfer credits toward the NYU Bachelor of Science degree in Communications Arts to students who complete this program.

The Audio and Video Electronics Technology program trains students for entry level positions as bench or field technicians doing audio and video repair work. The program can be completed full time in 6 months or part time in 9-12 months.

The Institute's student body regularly includes employees of broadcast and industrial companies, studios, and other concerns in the audio and video fields. Tours of the Institute's studio complex, laboratories, and other facilities can be arranged through their admissions office for individuals and groups.

School:	*Institute of Communication Arts*
Address:	*Suite 12 -12840 Bathgate Way* *Richmond, B.C.* *V6V 1Z4 CANADA*
Phone:	*604-278-0232*
Program Director:	*Niels Hartvig-Nielsen*
Admissions Director:	*Shannon B. Barker*
Programs Offered:	*Audio Recording, Music Technology, Video, Commercial Music Performance and Business, Electronic Music*
Program Length:	*1-2 years/6 week Accelerated Program*
Program Cost:	*variable*
Program Established:	*1979*
Accreditation:	*B.C. Ministry of Advanced Education*
Number of Studios:	*6*
Tracks per Studio:	*4-24*
Types of Recording:	*Analog, Digital, Video*
Average Class Size:	*1 +*
Main Emphasis of Program:	*Practical experience in equipment operations, plus business communication skills*
Additional Resources:	
Financial Aid	√
Scholarships	√
Professional Internships	√
Job Placement	√
Admission Policy:	*Highly selective*
Admission Prerequisites:	*High school diploma, good communication skills, references, intermediate music skills for music courses*

Classes Offered:

Analog Electronics	√	Digital Electronics	√
Physics		Acoustics	√
Music Theory	√	Music Performance	√
Microphone Techniques	√	Pure Stereo Techniques	
Equipment Maintenance	√	Equipment Alignment	√
Video Techniques	√	Film Techniques	√
Business/ Marketing	√	Legal Aspects of Recording	√
Electronic Music Synthesis	√	Computer/ MIDI Techniques	√
Sound Reinforcement	√	Audio System Design	

Profile:

Supporting the basic statement " you can't learn to fly in ground school," I.C.A. approaches education in a three step process- theory, example, and application. Many classes are actual sessions, initially in groups as small as three students with an instructor and eventually in non-instructional studio sessions assigned to individual students. Skills in art, techniques, and business are instructed in support of what is essentially a freelance industry; I.C.A.'s " in house " departments work together to simulate realistic industry. The Commercial Music Performance groups perform live, the event organized by business students, recorded by audio engineering students, and videotaped by the video department.

I.C.A. instructors work in the industry as good communicators and are supported by in-house teacher training instructor Terry Baker, author of " Bosstalk " and well known Canadian seminar leader. Also on the staff is David Miles Huber, co-author of " Modern Recording Techniques " and author of " Audio Production Techniques for Video " and " Microphones ". These texts and their authors contribute greatly to the international success of I.C.A.

New in 1989 is a combination home study/school attendance program which will see students purchase recording, computer, synthesizer, signal processing and video equipment as part of the study program. The student attends a reduced " on campus " study program in favour of practical experience at home. Students attend the more sophisticated "on campus" facilities to complete projects and gain experience with the advanced level of equipment after learning the basics at home on their own schedule.

Digital and automation will be the focus of a special SSL/Digital workshop program designed for advanced students and working engineers. The program will be held in Lahaina, Maui, and I.C.A. sponsored workshops will be held throughout the year. For further information contact the school.

School:	*Dave Kennedy Recording Studios*
Address:	*Recording School for Audio Engineers* *8006 W. Appleton Avenue* *Milwaukee, WI 53218*
Phone:	*414-527-3127*
Program Director:	*Dave Kennedy*
Admissions Director:	*Dave Kennedy*
Programs Offered:	*Audio Recording & Engineering*
Program Length:	*8 weeks*
Program Cost:	*$650*
Program Established:	*1973*
Accreditation:	*Wisconsin Department of Education*
Number of Studios:	*1*
Tracks per Studio:	*16*
Types of Recording:	*Analog*
Average Class Size:	*7*
Main Emphasis of Program:	*Hands-on training*
Additional Resources:	
Financial Aid	√
Scholarships	
Professional Internships	
Job Placement	
Admission Policy:	*Open*
Admission Prerequisites:	*High school diploma or equivalent*

Classes Offered:

Analog Electronics	√	Digital Electronics	√
Physics		Acoustics	√
Music Theory		Music Performance	
Microphone Techniques	√ ·	Pure Stereo Techniques	√
Equipment Maintenance	√	Equipment Alignment	√
Video Techniques		Film Techniques	
Business/ Marketing		Legal Aspects of Recording	√
Electronic Music Synthesis	√	Computer/ MIDI Techniques	
Sound Reinforcement	√	Audio System Design	√

Profile:

The Recording School for Audio Engineers at Dave Kennedy Recording Studios offers an eight week, 80 hour Basic Audio Recording and Engineering. The program meets twice weekly for five hours on Monday and Wednesday or Tuesday and Thursday.

Each meeting covers different audio recording related topics. Included in the course of study are discussions of sound and hearing, microphone types and techniques, console and tape machine operation for multitrack recording, recording and producing 30/60 second commercials, equalization and signal processing, and recording production of a full music ensemble. The course concludes with a final exam on all topics covered.

Dave Kennedy Recording Studios is also the largest full service audio recording facility in Wisconsin. Personal tours are available by appointment.

School:	*Koninklijk Conservatorium*
Address:	*Royal Conservatory*
	Juliana van Stolberglaan 1
	2595 CA The Hague HOLLAND
Phone:	*070-814251*
Program Director:	*Stan Tempelaars*
Admissions Director:	*Peter Nuyten*
Programs Offered:	*Music Recording - Sonology*
Program Length:	*4 years*
Program Cost:	*1,500 Dutch Guilders per year*
Program Established:	*1983*
Accreditation:	*University of Utrecht*
Number of Studios:	*2*
Tracks per Studio:	*8,16*
Types of Recording:	*Analog, Digital*
Average Class Size:	*15*
Main Emphasis of Program:	*Education of recording engineerings with highly developed musical skills*

Additional Resources:
Financial Aid
Scholarships
Professional Internships √
Job Placement

Admission Policy:	*Selective*
Admission Prerequisites:	*High school diploma with math and physics, musical training*

Classes Offered:

Analog Electronics	√	Digital Electronics	√
Physics	√	Acoustics	√
Music Theory	√	Music Performance	√
Microphone Techniques	√	Pure Stereo Techniques	√
Equipment Maintenance	√	Equipment Alignment	√
Video Techniques		Film Techniques	
Business/ Marketing	√	Legal Aspects of Recording	√
Electronic Music Synthesis	√	Computer/ MIDI Techniques	√
Sound Reinforcement	√	Audio System Design	√

Profile:

The Koninklijk Convervatorium offers a four year Music Engineering program consisting of a two year theoretical program of music and technology followed by a two year practical program.

The practical program offers a special training In either "Concert Hall Recording" or "Studio Recording". During this program, at least 20 different recording sessions are executed and edited or mixed to a final master product.

After completion of study, students have gained basic experience in organizing recording sessions, score editing, dubbing, sampling, and composing and arranging music.

Applicants should be aware that instrumental or vocal performance is part of the study and that the program is presented in the Dutch language. A separate one year course in the fundamentals of electronic music synthesis is also available and is presented in English.

School:	*Lincoln Institute*
Address:	*7622 Louette Road* *Spring, TX 77379*
Phone:	*713-376-9679*
Program Director:	*Joe E. Lincoln*
Admissions Director:	*Joy Kowalik*
Programs Offered:	*Audio Engineering and Video Production*
Program Length:	*18 months*
Program Cost:	*$6,600*
Program Established:	*1984*
Accreditation:	*Texas Education Agency*
Number of Studios:	*2*
Tracks per Studio:	*16*
Types of Recording:	*Analog, Video, Film*
Average Class Size:	*10*
Main Emphasis of Program:	*Hands-on training*

Additional Resources:
Financial Aid √
Scholarships
Professional Internships √
Job Placement

Admission Policy:	*Open*
Admission Prerequisites:	*High school diploma or GED*

Classes Offered:

Analog Electronics	√	Digital Electronics	√
Physics		Acoustics	√
Music Theory	√	Music Performance	
Microphone Techniques	√	Pure Stereo Techniques	√
Equipment Maintenance	√	Equipment Alignment	√
Video Techniques	√	Film Techniques	
Business/ Marketing	√	Legal Aspects of Recording	√
Electronic Music Synthesis	√	Computer/ MIDI Techniques	√
Sound Reinforcement	√	Audio System Design	√

Profile:

The Lincoln Institute offers 18 month programs in Audio Engineering and Video Production. The Audio Engineering program presents the student with a well-rounded overview of the recording industry and prepares the student for an entry level position in a recording related occupation. The curriculum exposes the student to courses in electronics, acoustic design, music theory and practice, and recording technology. The program's expanding technical facility exposes students to the type of recording hardware that they will encountered in the recording industry.

The Video Production program prepares students for entry level positions in television or film related occupations. The curriculum includes courses in set design, producing and directing, lighting, video recording, editing, and special effects graphics. The program is designed to prepare students for full time employment immediately upon completion of the entire course of study.

The Lincoln Institute maintains a broadcast quality television studio and a state of the art multitrack recording studio. This allows students the opportunity to gain maximum hands-on instruction in using recording machines, synthesizers, and automated production consoles. The television studio offers 1/2", 3/4", 1", and 2" production and includes digital recording modes with instant replay, time lapse, and slow motion effects.

General information bulletins are available from the school for $2.

School:	*Los Angeles City College*
Address:	*855 North Vermont Avenue* *Los Angeles, CA 90029*
Phone:	*213-669-5545*
Program Director:	*J. Robert Stahley*
Admissions Director:	*J. Robert Stahley*
Programs Offered:	*Radio, Television, Cinema, Recording*
Program Length:	*One 18 week semester each*
Program Cost:	*$50/semester California residents*
Program Established:	*1935*
Accreditation:	*WAC*
Number of Studios:	*6*
Tracks per Studio:	*8, 24, 32*
Types of Recording:	*Analog, Video, Film*
Average Class Size:	*25-30*
Main Emphasis of Program:	*Production*

Additional Resources:
Financial Aid √
Scholarships √
Professional Internships √
Job Placement

Admission Policy:	*Open*
Admission Prerequisites:	*18 years old, California resident for one yea.* *non-residents pay additional fee*

Classes Offered:

Analog Electronics		Digital Electronics
Physics		Acoustics
Music Theory	√	Music Performance
Microphone Techniques	√	Pure Stereo Techniques
Equipment Maintenance	√	Equipment Alignment
Video Techniques	√	Film Techniques √
Business/ Marketing	√	Legal Aspects of Recording √
Electronic Music Synthesis		Computer/ MIDI Techniques
Sound Reinforcement		Audio System Design

Profile:

The Radio-Television-Film Department at Los Angeles City College offers students comprehensive programs that provide both basic and advanced courses in the latest studio and field production techniques using state of the art equipment.

For Cinema, there is a fully equipped film sound stage, 26 editing suites, three screening room, plus full audio post-production and animation facilities. In addition, these is extensive 16mm production equipment available to all students.

For Television, there are two complete, broadcast quality color television studios. An elaborate master control connects the studios as well as the off-line video editing suites. Remote equipment is available for electronic field production and news gather.

For Radio, there are modern post-production facilities, including 18 radio production rooms for producing shows for the school's on-air broadcast station. The Recording Arts program utilizes 8 and 24 track studios for recording live performances.

The department's faculty and staff consists of over two dozen professionals, engineers and educators who provide expert technical advice combined with detailed information on current industry procedures.

With no prior experience required, students begin hands-on production in their first semester. They then advance to courses that prepare them for employment in the industry. Students are eligible for the Associate of Arts degree and can also receive a certificate of completion in their chosen areas of specialization.

School:	*Los Angeles Harbor College*
Address:	*Recording Studio*
	1111 Figueroa Place
	Wilmington, CA 90744
Phone:	*213-518-1000 ext. 235*
Program Director:	*John Payne*
Admissions Director:	*Bob Billings*
Programs Offered:	*Certificate in Recording Arts*
Program Length:	*2 years*
Program Cost:	*$50/semester California residents*
Program Established:	*1979*
Accreditation:	*Los Angeles Community College System*
Number of Studios:	*1*
Tracks per Studio:	*16*
Types of Recording:	*Analog*
Average Class Size:	*15-30 lecture, 5 labs*
Main Emphasis of Program:	*Multitrack studio recording*

Additional Resources:
Financial Aid
Scholarships
Professional Internships
Job Placement

Admission Policy:	*Open*
Admission Prerequisites:	*High school diploma preferred*

Classes Offered:

Analog Electronics	√	Digital Electronics	√
Physics	√	Acoustics	√
Music Theory	√	Music Performance	√
Microphone Techniques	√	Pure Stereo Techniques	√
Equipment Maintenance		Equipment Alignment	√
Video Techniques	√	Film Techniques	
Business/ Marketing	√	Legal Aspects of Recording	
Electronic Music Synthesis	√	Computer/ MIDI Techniques	√
Sound Reinforcement		Audio System Design	

Profile:

The Recording Arts program at Los Angeles Harbor College offers quality, low cost training for work in the music and recording industries.

The core program consists of four consecutive semesters of Recording Arts courses, with hands-on studio beginning after the first semester. The optional Recording Arts Certificate in Commercial Music is available to students who take additional courses in electronic music theory and practice and music theory and performance, for a total of 40 units or about 15 courses. Transfer credits are also accepted, if they are equivalent to recommended courses.

Students have individual and small group access to a fully professional multitrack studio, featuring 3M-79 16 track and 2 track recorders, a 20 x16 recording console, various outboard equipment, and microphones by AKG, Neumann, Shure, and others.

School:	*Los Angeles Recording Workshop*
Address:	*12268 Ventura Blvd* *Studio City, CA 91604*
Phone:	*818-763-7400*
Program Director:	*Christopher Knight*
Admissions Director:	*Ivana Zeri*
Programs Offered:	*Recording Engineering*
Program Length:	*200 hours per program*
Program Cost:	*$1,650*
Program Established:	*1984*
Accreditation:	*California Department of Education*
Number of Studios:	*6*
Tracks per Studio:	*One-16, Four-24*
Types of Recording:	*Analog, Digital*
Average Class Size:	*6 - 8*
Main Emphasis of Program:	*Job training*

Additional Resources:
Financial Aid
Scholarships
Professional Internships √
Job Placement √

Admission Policy:	*Open*
Admission Prerequisites:	*Open to anyone seriously interested in recording industry careers.*

Classes Offered:

Analog Electronics	√	Digital Electronics	√
Physics	√	Acoustics	√
Music Theory	√	Music Performance	
Microphone Techniques	√	Pure Stereo Techniques	√
Equipment Maintenance	√	Equipment Alignment	√
Video Techniques		Film Techniques	
Business/ Marketing	√	Legal Aspects of Recording	√
Electronic Music Synthesis	√	Computer/ MIDI Techniques	√
Sound Reinforcement	√	Audio System Design	√

Profile:

The Los Angeles Recording Workshop Recording Engineering Program is designed specifically to train students as professional studio recording engineers. Their program assumes that new students may not know anything about recording, but have the desire to know everything about recording.

Students train hands-on in six different studios: four different 24 track studios, one 16 track SPMTE-MIDI recording studio, and one rehearsal studio. Half of the training is done in small group (6-8 students) hands-on recording sessions.

The program's curriculum is complete and is approved for job training by the California Department of Education. Upon graduation students receive the Los Angeles Recording Workshop Certificate of Completion. An active internship and job placement program is provided for graduates and dorm housing is available for students.

A free catalog and soundsheet is available from the school's admissions office.

School:	*Los Medanos College*
Address:	*2700 E. Leland Road*
	Pittsburgh, CA 94565
Phone:	*415-439-0200*
Program Director:	*Frank Dorritie*
Admissions Director:	*John Walker*
Programs Offered:	*A.A. in Music/ Recording Arts*
	Recording Arts Certificate
Program Length:	*2 years*
Program Cost:	*$50/semester California residents*
Program Established:	*1979*
Accreditation:	*California Community Colleges*
Number of Studios:	*3*
Tracks per Studio:	*2, 4, 16*
Types of Recording:	*Analog, Digital*
Average Class Size:	*22*
Main Emphasis of Program:	*Preparation for job market*

Additional Resources:
Financial Aid √
Scholarships √
Professional Internships √
Job Placement √

Admission Policy:	*Open*
Admission Prerequisites:	*Desire to excel, willingness to work, skills*
	assessment test for placement

Classes Offered:

Analog Electronics	√	Digital Electronics	√
Physics		Acoustics	√
Music Theory	√	Music Performance	√
Microphone Techniques	√	Pure Stereo Techniques	
Equipment Maintenance	√	Equipment Alignment	√
Video Techniques	√	Film Techniques	
Business/ Marketing	√	Legal Aspects of Recording	√
Electronic Music Synthesis	√	Computer/ MIDI Techniques	√
Sound Reinforcement	√	Audio System Design	√

Profile:

The Recording Arts program at Los Medanos is the only one of its kind in northern California. interdisciplinary in nature, the curriculum is designed and taught by industry professionals and include courses in music, electrical engineering, physical science, mathematics, and business. Students in the program are given hands-on experience in multitrack recording, sound reinforcement, acoustics, MIDI, producing, and troubleshooting.

Present members of the Los Medanos College's Recording Arts faculty have received 11 Grammy nominations and 2 Grammy awards from the National Academy of Recording Arts and Sciences for their work in producing, songwriting, engineering, and performance.

School:	*Loyola Marymount University*
Address:	*Dept. of Communications*
	Los Angeles, CA 90045
Phone:	*213-642-3033*
Program Director:	*Vinay Shrivastava*
Admissions Director:	*Vinay Shrivastava*
Programs Offered:	*B.A. in Recording Arts*
Program Length:	*4 years*
Program Cost:	*$7,908 per year*
Program Established:	*1984*
Accreditation:	*Western Association of Schools and Colleges, California State Board of Education*
Number of Studios:	*7*
Tracks per Studio:	*4, 8, 16, 24*
Types of Recording:	*Analog, Digital, Video, Film*
Average Class Size:	*10-15*
Main Emphasis of Program:	*Multitrack recording, film, video*

Additional Resources:

Financial Aid	√
Scholarships	√
Professional Internships	√
Job Placement	√

Admission Policy:	*Selective*
Admission Prerequisites:	*High school diploma or GED, SAT scores, references*

Classes Offered:

Analog Electronics	√	Digital Electronics	
Physics	√	Acoustics	√
Music Theory	√	Music Performance	√
Microphone Techniques	√	Pure Stereo Techniques	√
Equipment Maintenance	√	Equipment Alignment	
Video Techniques	√	Film Techniques	√
Business/ Marketing	√	Legal Aspects of Recording	√
Electronic Music Synthesis	√	Computer/ MIDI Techniques	
Sound Reinforcement	√	Audio System Design	

Profile:

The program at Loyola is designed to provide a full spectrum of knowledge related to recording. Within the liberal arts curriculum of the university, Recording Arts provides both academic and pre-professional training to aspiring artists, engineers, producers, and sound designers. Courses offer a wide range of recording environments, including studio recording and mixing; motion picture production recording, sound design, effects, and post-production recording; recording for television; and music video production.

Content stresses both a theoretical and technical understanding of the field. Practical knowledge is developed through emphasizing hands-on experience with professional equipment. The curriculum also includes visits to working recording studios, record plants, and soundstages within the Los Angeles area. Distinguished professional from the recording and music industries are often featured as guest speakers In classes.

At Loyola, the Recording Arts program is part of the Communication Arts Division, which includes fields of study in Motion Picture Production, Television, Screenwriting, Media Studies, and Speech. As a result, students have access to the department's 60 x 90 cinema soundstage, 30 x 60 television studio with audio booth, Nagra tape recorders, and an FM stereo radio station- KXLU.

Students can enroll in related courses offered by other campus departments such as Music, Business, and Engineering. Loyola also makes available a number of internships with various studios and recording companies, providing the opportunity for students to learn and work in professional situations.

School:	***Miami Sunset Senior High School***
Address:	*13125 S.W. 72nd Street* *Miami, FL 33183*
Phone:	*305-385-4255 ext. 248*
Program Director:	*Daniel Sell*
Admissions Director:	*Daniel Sell*
Programs Offered:	*Audio Engineering,* *Television Production*
Program Length:	*1-3 years*
Program Cost:	*None to full time students*
Program Established:	*1982*
Accreditation:	*SASS*
Number of Studios:	*1*
Tracks per Studio:	*8*
Types of Recording:	*Analog*
Average Class Size:	*20*
Main Emphasis of Program:	*Preparation for college or trade school*

Additional Resources:
Financial Aid
Scholarships
Professional Internships
Job Placement

Admission Policy:	*Highly selective*
Admission Prerequisites:	*Interest, grade point average, references,* *interview with instructor*

Classes Offered:

Analog Electronics	√	Digital Electronics	
Physics	√	Acoustics	√
Music Theory	√	Music Performance	√
Microphone Techniques	√	Pure Stereo Techniques	
Equipment Maintenance		Equipment Alignment	
Video Techniques	√	Film Techniques	
Business/ Marketing		Legal Aspects of Recording	
Electronic Music Synthesis	√	Computer/ MIDI Techniques	
Sound Reinforcement	√	Audio System Design	√

Profile:

Miami Sunset Senior High School offers a three year curriculum in television production and recording engineering. Students in TV work in a four camera color studio with computer assisted editing, telecine, and interformat dubbing. Students produce commercials, live closed circuit broadcasts, daily news, and record schoolwide events, including four camera remotes.

Students involved in audio use an 8 track studio complete with noise reduction and outboard signal processing. Students also study sound reinforcement using the department's PA system.

Most projects include combining the TV, recording, and sound reinforcement equipment. These programs are open to all full-time students in the school.

School:	*Middle Tennessee State University*
Address:	*Box 21*
	Murfreesboro, TN 37132
Phone:	*615-898-2813*
Program Director:	*Geoffrey Hull*
Admissions Director:	*Dr. Rick Parrent*
Programs Offered:	*Bachelor of Science in Recording Industry Management*
Program Length:	*4 years*
Program Cost:	*$571/semester Tennessee residents, $1,939/semester non-residents*
Program Established:	*1973*
Accreditation:	*SACS*
Number of Studios:	*2*
Tracks per Studio:	*16,24*
Types of Recording:	*Analog, Digital, Video*
Average Class Size:	*15 lab*
Main Emphasis of Program:	*Music business and audio*
Additional Resources:	
Financial Aid	√
Scholarships	√
Professional Internships	√
Job Placement	√
Admission Policy:	*Open*
Admission Prerequisites:	*High school diploma, ACT composite of 17, SAT combined score of 825, or a 2.0 high school average*

Classes Offered:

Analog Electronics	√	Digital Electronics	√
Physics	√	Acoustics	√
Music Theory	√	Music Performance	√
Microphone Techniques	√	Pure Stereo Techniques	√
Equipment Maintenance	√	Equipment Alignment	√
Video Techniques	√	Film Techniques	
Business/ Marketing	√	Legal Aspects of Recording	√
Electronic Music Synthesis	√	Computer/ MIDI Techniques	√
Sound Reinforcement	√	Audio System Design	

Profile:

The Recording Industry Management program at Middle Tennessee State University is one of the largest and most successful college programs preparing students for careers in the music business and the audio recording industry. Located just 30 miles from Nashville, the program has over 400 majors, six full time faculty, and two multitrack recording studios. The newest studio is a 24 track digital studio with Sony multitrack and DAT machines, digital editing, and a Reflection Free Zone monitoring environment designed by award-winning consultant Bob Todrank.

Students in the program take a variety of courses dealing with both the business and audio aspects of the industry and then further concentrate their studies with advanced audio or additional specialized courses in the music business. Advanced audio courses include Advanced Technology of Recording, Digital Recording, Acoustics and Maintenance, Studio Production, and Studio Administration. Business courses include Promotion and Publicity, Concert Promotion/Production, and Record Store Operations. An extensive internship program provides students in their junior and senior years with opportunities to work in virtually any phase of the industry.

In addition to 36 semester hours in the major, students have a required minor in Mass Communications and a second minor required in either Business Administration, Electronics, or Music Industry. Over 35% of the students in the program are from outside Tennessee, and over half of the students transfer to Middle Tennessee State University from other schools.

School:	***Millikin University***
Address:	*1184 West Main*
	Decatur, IL 62522
Phone:	*217-424-6254*
Program Director:	*A. Wesley Tower*
Admissions Director:	*Wallace Barnett*
Programs Offered:	*Bachelor of Music in Commercial Music*
Program Length:	*4 years*
Program Cost:	*Approx. $10,000 per year*
Program Established:	*1980*
Accreditation:	*NASM*
Number of Studios:	*1*
Tracks per Studio:	*24*
Types of Recording:	*Analog*
Average Class Size:	*25*
Main Emphasis of Program:	*Performance*

Additional Resources:
Financial Aid √
Scholarships √
Professional Internships
Job Placement

Admission Policy:	*Selective*
Admission Prerequisites:	*Music audition*

Classes Offered:

Analog Electronics		Digital Electronics	
Physics		Acoustics	
Music Theory	√	Music Performance	√
Microphone Techniques	√	Pure Stereo Techniques	
Equipment Maintenance		Equipment Alignment	
Video Techniques		Film Techniques	
Business/ Marketing	√	Legal Aspects of Recording	
Electronic Music Synthesis		Computer/ MIDI Techniques	
Sound Reinforcement		Audio System Design	

Profile:

Millikin University was the first accredited university in the Midwest to offer a Bachelor of Music degree program in Commercial Music with a vocal and instrumental emphasis. In addition to the traditional aspects of professional music training, course concentration includes Commercial Music Performance, Commercial Music Arranging, Commercial Music Ensembles, Traditional and Commercial Studio Ensembles, Recording Studio Engineering, Record Producing, Jingle Writing, Commercial Vocal Styles, Commercial Music Theory, improvisation Techniques, and Commercial/Jazz History and Forms.

School:	*New York University*
Address:	*Dept. of Music & Music Education*
	35 West 4th Street, Room 777
	New York, NY 10003
Phone:	*212-998-5424*
Program Director:	*David Sanders*
Admissions Director:	*David Sanders*
Programs Offered:	*Bachelor of Music in Music Business &*
	Technology
Program Length:	*4 year*
Program Cost:	*$8,700*
Program Established:	*1978*
Accreditation:	*NASM*
Number of Studios:	*8*
Tracks per Studio:	*4, 8, 16*
Types of Recording:	*Analog, Video*
Average Class Size:	*8-25*
Main Emphasis of Program:	*Musical applications of technology and*
	equipment
Additional Resources:	
Financial Aid	√
Scholarships	√
Professional Internships	√
Job Placement	√
Admission Policy:	*Highly selective*
Admission Prerequisites:	*High school diploma, SAT, music audition,*
	interview

Classes Offered:

Analog Electronics	√	Digital Electronics	
Physics	√	Acoustics	√
Music Theory	√	Music Performance	√
Microphone Techniques	√	Pure Stereo Techniques	
Equipment Maintenance	√	Equipment Alignment	√
Video Techniques	√	Film Techniques	
Business/ Marketing	√	Legal Aspects of Recording	√
Electronic Music Synthesis	√	Computer/ MIDI Techniques	√
Sound Reinforcement		Audio System Design	

Profile:

New York University offers specialized courses in Analog Synthesis, Computer Music, FM Synthesis, MIDI, Electronic Music Composition, Film Scoring, Studio Production, and Audio Engineering. Four year programs lead to Bachelor of Music degrees in Music Business and Technology, Composition, Performance, Jazz Studies, and Music Education. Non-degree, special-student status is available to those wishing to enroll only in specific classes. Graduate studies leading to M.A., D.A., Ed.D., and Ph.D. degrees are also offered.

NYU recording and electronic music studios are continually being upgraded. Current facilities include a 16 track recording studio, three 8 track studios, and two 4 track studios. All are MIDI equipped with computers (IBM, Atari, Macintosh, Amiga, and Yamaha), a varied selection of synthesizers (Yamaha, Korg, Fairlight, Voyetra, McClavier, Arp, Buchla, and Serge), mixers, monitoring systems, and a wide assortment of outboard gear.

Research laboratories provide opportunities for application of Computer and MIDI in music education and music therapy. Advanced techniques in digital synthesis and computer aided composition are explored utilizing the school's DEC PDP11-44 computer system.

School:	*Northest Community College*
Address:	*801 E. Benjamin Avenue*
	Norfolk, NE 68701
Phone:	*402-371-2020*
Program Director:	*Timothy Miller*
Admissions Director:	*Gene Hart*
Programs Offered:	*A.A. in Audio Recording Technology*
Program Length:	*2 years*
Program Cost:	*$21/credit Nebraska residents,*
	$29/credit non-residents
Program Established:	*1981*
Accreditation:	*NCAC*
Number of Studios:	*2*
Tracks per Studio:	*8, 16*
Types of Recording:	*Analog, Digital*
Average Class Size:	*10-20*
Main Emphasis of Program:	*Employment preparation*

Additional Resources:
Financial Aid √
Scholarships √
Professional Internships √
Job Placement √

Admission Policy:	*Open*
Admission Prerequisites:	*High school diploma or GED*

Classes Offered:

Analog Electronics	√	Digital Electronics	√
Physics	√	Acoustics	√
Music Theory	√	Music Performance	√
Microphone Techniques	√	Pure Stereo Techniques	√
Equipment Maintenance	√	Equipment Alignment	√
Video Techniques	√	Film Techniques	
Business/ Marketing	√	Legal Aspects of Recording	√
Electronic Music Synthesis	√	Computer/ MIDI Techniques	√
Sound Reinforcement	√	Audio System Design	

Profile:

Northeast Community College offers quality education in a friendly rural community of 20,000 located in northeast Nebraska. Small class size, personal attention, and affordability are keystones of education at Northeast.

The Audio and Recording Technology curriculum offers a two year associate degree that provides theoretical and hands-on education in audio and recording, electronics, music, and classes related to completing a well round program. The audio program has continued its growth with the recent addition of digital mastering and a professional, portable concert sound reinforcement system.

School:	***Omega Studios' School of Applied Recording Arts & Sciences***
Address:	*Omega Recording Studios*
	5609 Fishers Lane
	Rockville, MD 20852
Phone:	*301-230-9100*
Program Director:	*W. Robert Yesbek*
Admissions Director:	*Betty Phelps*
Programs Offered:	*Basic, Intermediate, Advanced Studio Techniques, Advertising Production, MIDI*
Program Length:	*6-10 weeks per program*
Program Cost:	*$595-$995*
Program Established:	*1977*
Accreditation:	*Maryland Department of Education, American University*
Number of Studios:	*4*
Tracks per Studio:	*2, 4, 8, 24, 48*
Types of Recording:	*Analog, Digital*
Average Class Size:	*8-20 lecture, 4-6 workshops*
Main Emphasis of Program:	*Studio engineering techniques and electronic music*
Additional Resources:	
Financial Aid	
Scholarships	
Professional Internships	
Job Placement	√
Admission Policy:	*Open*
Admission Prerequisites:	*None for intro courses*

Classes Offered:

Analog Electronics		Digital Electronics	
Physics	√	Acoustics	√
Music Theory		Music Performance	
Microphone Techniques	√	Pure Stereo Techniques	√
Equipment Maintenance	√	Equipment Alignment	√
Video Techniques		Film Techniques	
Business/ Marketing		Legal Aspects of Recording	
Electronic Music Synthesis	√	Computer/ MIDI Techniques	√
Sound Reinforcement	√	Audio System Design	

Profile:

The Omega Studios' School of Applied Recording Arts & Sciences operates out of the facilities of Omega Recording Studios in suburban Washington, D.C. This four studio complex offers 24 and 48 track recording in its largest studio- A; 24 track in studio B; 2, 4, 8 track radio, TV, industrial, and educational audio production in studio C, and a complete MIDI setup in studio D. Founded in1977, the school also offers academic credit for students enrolled in The American University in Washington, D.C.

The Basic program covers acoustics, microphone techniques, signal processing, tape machine theory and alignment, console theory and signal flow, mixing for CD and record production, and features hands-on classes in session techniques and mixing. The Intermediate program centers around hands-on operation of the equipment and familiarizes the student with the various consoles and machines at Omega. The Advanced class centers around specific subjects such as audio for video interlock, basic MIDI control room interface, advanced acoustics, advanced production techniques, and hands-on operation of signal processors.

The Recording Techniques for Advertising program follows the production of a jingle from multitrack to final voiceovers. The student will leave with a complete understanding of the jingle/voice-over process. The Basic and Advanced MIDI programs familiarize the student with the MIDI-lock process on a computer synthesizer/ sequencer system. The Advanced program offers intensive hands-on instruction.

Omega's course director designed and teaches similar programs at the American University and is on the Faculty Advisory Committees for Montgomery College and Anne Arundel College. This, along with Omega's day to day contact with the " real world " of recording allows the student to get a realistic picture of the field while still maintaining a basic familiarity with the theories and science involved.

School:	*Ontario Institute of Audio Recording Technology*
Address:	*500 Newbold Street*
	London, Ontario N6E 1K6
	CANADA
Phone:	*519-686-5010*
Program Director:	*Peter Kryshtalovich*
Admissions Director:	*Geoff Keymer*
Programs Offered:	*Audio Recording Technologies*
Program Length:	*8 months*
Program Cost:	*$4,250 Canadian funds*
Program Established:	*1983*
Accreditation:	*Ontario Ministry of College and Universities*
Number of Studios:	*2*
Tracks per Studio:	*24*
Types of Recording:	*Analog, Digital, Video, MIDI*
Average Class Size:	*20-25 lecture, 3-4 labs*
Main Emphasis of Program:	*Theoretical and practical skill development in all aspects of audio recording*

Additional Resources:
Financial Aid √
Scholarships
Professional Internships √
Job Placement √

Admission Policy: *Open*

Admission Prerequisites: *18 years of age, secondary school diploma or mature sudent status. Experience in music and or audio technology is recommended, but is not a prerequisite.*

Classes Offered:

Analog Electronics	√	Digital Electronics	√
Physics	√	Acoustics	√
Music Theory	√	Music Performance	√
Microphone Techniques	√	Pure Stereo Techniques	√
Equipment Maintenance	√	Equipment Alignment	√
Video Techniques	√	Film Techniques	
Business/ Marketing	√	Legal Aspects of Recording	√
Electronic Music Synthesis	√	Computer/ MIDI Techniques	√
Sound Reinforcement	√	Audio System Design	√

Profile:

The Ontario Institute of Audio Recording Technology was established in 1983 with one fundamental intent- to quickly and efficiently fulfill the educational needs of those with career aspirations in the audio recording industry. The directors of the school have implemented an intensely focused program of study which is completed within one academic year. The individual always comes first at OIART- enrollment is intentionally restricted to approximately 50 students per year, and there are seven full time instructors who provide qualified guidance and support. Streamlined courses, state of the art equipment, and a staff well acquainted with all aspects of the industry combine to make OIART an exceptional facility in which to learn.

Courses of instruction begin at an introductory level and accelerate rapidly, combing to provide the student with knowledge and practical skills in all aspects of audio recording, including management, music production, video, acoustics, microphone use, tape recorders, mixing consoles, monitoring systems, signal processors, and much more. Designed in close liaison with the music/recording industry, the program emphasizes concentrated practical experience and theoretical training training that the student will require in order to become a qualified engineer. Though the program stresses the technical recording aspects of the music business, the student is at all time reminded that we deal with a creative industry and is encourages to engage in performance, composition, and songwriting.

The course is a step-through process with a simple beginning- wrapping cables. Smaller concepts and skills build on each other until, within five months, students are creatively and responsibly operating a $300,000 recording facility. By mid-February, each individual is pursuing projects of their choice and is encourage to develop a portfolio that accurately represents their career aspirations.

OIART studio equipment represents technology found in every major recording facility, worldwide. Students use equipment from Mitsubishi, Sony, Studer, Lexicon, JVC, Roland, MCI, AKG, Yamaha, Neumann, Sennheiser, Adams-Smith, Urei, Keypex, and Hybrid Arts.

School:	*Peabody Institute- Conservatory of Music*
Address:	*John Hopkins University*
	1 East Mount Vernon Place
	Baltimore, MD 21202-2397
Phone:	*301-659-8110 or 800-368-2521*
Program Director:	*Alan Kefauver*
Admissions Director:	*David Lane*
Programs Offered:	*Bachelor of Music in Recording Arts and Sciences*
Program Length:	*5 years*
Program Cost:	*$9,100*
Program Established:	*1980*
Accreditation:	*NASM, Maryland Department of Education*
Number of Studios:	*2*
Tracks per Studio:	*24*
Types of Recording:	*Analog, Digital*
Average Class Size:	*<10*
Main Emphasis of Program:	*Music and technology*

Additional Resources:
  Financial Aid √
  Scholarships √
  Professional Internships √
  Job Placement √

Admission Policy:	*Highly selective*
Admission Prerequisites:	*High school diploma, high SAT scores, musical audition*

Classes Offered:

Analog Electronics	√	Digital Electronics	√
Physics	√	Acoustics	√
Music Theory	√	Music Performance	√
Microphone Techniques	√	Pure Stereo Techniques	√
Equipment Maintenance	√	Equipment Alignment	√
Video Techniques	√	Film Techniques	
Business/ Marketing		Legal Aspects of Recording	
Electronic Music Synthesis	√	Computer/ MIDI Techniques	√
Sound Reinforcement	√	Audio System Design	√

Profile:

This Recording Arts and Sciences program was conceived as an American counterpart to the European "Tonmeister" training, and draws its strengths from the engineering programs of the G.W.C. Whiting School of Engineering of the John Hopkins University and the entire theory and performance curriculum of the Peabody Conservatory of Music.

The course of study includes completion of a Bachelor of Music degree program at Peabody, which makes up the first of the two degrees in this five year, double degree program. Students also complete approximately one third of the Electrical Engineering program at The John Hopkins University, which, combined with the Recording curriculum at Peabody makes up the second of the two degrees.

Applicants must demonstrate ability in both degree areas. Therefore, a performance audition of conservatory entrance level is required, as well as an academic background showing strength in math and science.

School:	**Penn State University**
Address:	*220 Special Services Building University Park, PA 16802*
Phone:	*814-863-2911*
Program Director:	*Peter Kiefer*
Admissions Director:	*Peter Kiefer*
Programs Offered:	*Sound Recording Workshop*
Program Length:	*3-4 days*
Program Cost:	*$137 Pennsylvania residents, $205 non-residents*
Program Established:	*1980*
Accreditation:	
Number of Studios:	*4*
Tracks per Studio:	*2 - 4*
Types of Recording:	*Analog, Video*
Average Class Size:	*25*
Main Emphasis of Program:	*Practical working knowledge of audio systems*
Additional Resources: Financial Aid Scholarships Professional Internships Job Placement	
Admission Policy:	*Open*
Admission Prerequisites:	*None*

Classes Offered:

Analog Electronics		Digital Electronics	
Physics		Acoustics	
Music Theory		Music Performance	
Microphone Techniques	√	Pure Stereo Techniques	√
Equipment Maintenance		Equipment Alignment	√
Video Techniques		Film Techniques	
Business/ Marketing		Legal Aspects of Recording	
Electronic Music Synthesis		Computer/ MIDI Techniques	
Sound Reinforcement	√	Audio System Design	√

Profile:

The Penn State University four day Workshop is a practical course for music teachers, directors, young people, and others seeking experience in and knowledge about sound amplification and recording. Participants receive practical information that will help them select and operate equipment to achieve optimum performance. Workshop sessions are held In Eisenhower Auditorium and in the WPSX-TV studios on the Penn State University Park campus.

Topics covered include: microphones, mixers, amplifiers, speakers, and recorders; sound reinforcement, concert setup techniques, types of equipment necessary for concerts and recording sessions, and hands-on experience in live concert situations.

School:	*RBY Recording and Video*
Address:	*920 North Main Street*
	Southbury, CT 06488
Phone:	*203-264-3666*
Program Director:	*Jack Jones*
Admissions Director:	*Marjorie Jones*
Programs Offered:	*Basic Multitrack Recording,*
	Basic Video Production
Program Length:	*18 hours*
Program Cost:	*$650*
Program Established:	*1977*
Accreditation:	*None*
Number of Studios:	*2*
Tracks per Studio:	*24*
Types of Recording:	*Analog, Digital, Video*
Average Class Size:	*1 - 2*
Main Emphasis of Program:	*General studio procedures*

Additional Resources:
Financial Aid
Scholarships
Professional Internships
Job Placement

Admission Policy:	*Selective*
Admission Prerequisites:	*Strong desire to continue in the industry and*
	education

Classes Offered:

Analog Electronics		Digital Electronics	
Physics		Acoustics	
Music Theory		Music Performance	
Microphone Techniques	√	Pure Stereo Techniques	
Equipment Maintenance	√	Equipment Alignment	√
Video Techniques	√	Film Techniques	
Business/ Marketing		Legal Aspects of Recording	
Electronic Music Synthesis		Computer/ MIDI Techniques	
Sound Reinforcement		Audio System Design	

Profile:

The purpose of RBY's program is to provide a way for students to decide if the audio/video field suits them. By getting a complete overview in RBY's comprehensive course, the individual is provided the opportunity to see if they are intellectually and emotionally geared to the recording profession.

School:	*Recording Arts Program of Canada*
Address:	*28 Valrose Drive*
	Stoney Creek, Ontario
	L8E 3T4 CANADA
Phone:	*416-662-2666*
Program Director:	*Nick Keca*
Admissions Director:	*Nick Keca*
Programs Offered:	*Recording Engineering, Music Production, Post-production Audio*
Program Length:	*13 weeks*
Program Cost:	*$1,700*
Program Established:	*1984*
Accreditation:	*Ontario Ministry of Colleges and Universities*
Number of Studios:	*3*
Tracks per Studio:	*16, 24*
Types of Recording:	*Analog, Digital, Video*
Average Class Size:	*7*
Main Emphasis of Program:	*Practical skills*
Additional Resources:	
Financial Aid	√
Scholarships	
Professional Internships	
Job Placement	√
Admission Policy:	*Selective*
Admission Prerequisites:	*High school diploma or mature student status*

Classes Offered:

Analog Electronics	√	Digital Electronics	√
Physics		Acoustics	√
Music Theory		Music Performance	
Microphone Techniques	√	Pure Stereo Techniques	√
Equipment Maintenance	√	Equipment Alignment	√
Video Techniques	√	Film Techniques	√
Business/ Marketing	√	Legal Aspects of Recording	√
Electronic Music Synthesis	√	Computer/ MIDI Techniques	√
Sound Reinforcement	√	Audio System Design	√

Profile:

The focus of the Recording Arts Program of Canada is almost exclusively on recording engineering and production. Initially, students learn the fundamentals of the recording process through theoretical instruction, augmented by practical activities. As the students become more familiar and comfortable with the technology, the balance shifts towards practical instruction, In general, there are two hours of formal instruction in a classroom setting for every three hours spent in the recording studio or computer music suite.

A critical component of the Recording Arts Program of Canada is maintaining a state of the art facility. The school feels that by moving in step with the commercial community, and presenting an environment that encourages a comprehensive and practical understanding of various production techniques, along with a fluent command of the technology, they will be developing student skills and tools that will extend beyond school into the students' working lives.

In brief, the school's scope of instruction includes: recording engineering, production techniques, computer music, digital technology, music business, acoustic principles, and post-production audio.

Classes are assembled according to student's academic, musical, and technical background, with no more than seven students per class. This format allows each class to establish an appropriate pace and encourages a great deal of personal attention.

School:	*Recording Associates*
Address:	*5821 S.E. Powell Boulevard* *Portland, OR 97206*
Phone:	*503-777-4621*
Program Director:	*Jay Webster*
Admissions Director:	*Jay Webster*
Programs Offered:	*Level 100, Level 150, Internship in Sound and Recording Technology*
Program Length:	*30-500 hours*
Program Cost:	*$250, $895, $2,950*
Program Established:	*1978*
Accreditation:	*Oregon Department of Vocational Education*
Number of Studios:	*2*
Tracks per Studio:	*16, 24*
Types of Recording:	*Analog*
Average Class Size:	*1 - 2*
Main Emphasis of Program:	*Sound recording*
Additional Resources: Financial Aid Scholarships Professional Internships Job Placement	
Admission Policy:	*Open*
Admission Prerequisites:	*None*

Classes Offered:

Analog Electronics		Digital Electronics	
Physics		Acoustics	√
Music Theory		Music Performance	
Microphone Techniques	√	Pure Stereo Techniques	
Equipment Maintenance	√	Equipment Alignment	√
Video Techniques		Film Techniques	
Business/ Marketing		Legal Aspects of Recording	
Electronic Music Synthesis		Computer/ MIDI Techniques	√
Sound Reinforcement	√	Audio System Design	

Profile:

Recording Associates offers several courses in sound and recording technology. Among them are the Level 100, Level 150, and Internship programs that provide varying numbers of courses within each curriculum.

The Level 100 program covers basic recording language and theory, technology and equipment, and practical methods, providing an introduction to the beginning student. Level 150 is a continuation of the studies begun in Level 100 and consists of four separate areas of concentration: sound awareness, tone awareness, multi channel mix control, and practical application. The practical application area includes practice recording sessions and studio time for the student's personal projects.

Recording Associates' most complete program of study is their six month Internship that can be taken either full or part time. The program consists of 21 separate courses including the Level 100 and 150 courses. Students participate in every aspect of the recording studio in this program and also gain experience in duplication, editing, and business contact. This program allows students to do several personal recording projects and charge their clients, if the student so desires.

Recording Associates also offers several instructional videos on recording related topics, including The Essentials of Drum Sounds, MIDI, SMPTE, and three separate programs on Sound Recording and Mixing.

School:	*Recording Institute*
Address:	*14511 Delano Street* *Van Nuys, CA 91411*
Phone:	*213-254-1756*
Program Director:	*Larry B. Cook*
Admissions Director:	*Larry B. Cook*
Programs Offered:	*Recording Engineering*
Program Length:	*8-9 months*
Program Cost:	*$6,000-$6,500*
Program Established:	*1987*
Accreditation:	*California Department of Education*
Number of Studios:	*1*
Tracks per Studio:	*24*
Types of Recording:	*Analog, Video*
Average Class Size:	*8*
Main Emphasis of Program:	*Hands-on music recording*
Additional Resources:	
Financial Aid	√
Scholarships	
Professional Internships	√
Job Placement	√
Admission Policy:	*Highly selective*
Admission Prerequisites:	*High school diploma*

Classes Offered:

Analog Electronics	√	Digital Electronics	√
Physics		Acoustics	√
Music Theory	√	Music Performance	
Microphone Techniques	√	Pure Stereo Techniques	
Equipment Maintenance	√	Equipment Alignment	√
Video Techniques	√	Film Techniques	
Business/ Marketing		Legal Aspects of Recording	
Electronic Music Synthesis	√	Computer/ MIDI Techniques	√
Sound Reinforcement	√	Audio System Design	

Profile:

The Recording Institute offers a Recording Specialist program that consists of 520 clock hours of instruction and application. The program requires 7-8 months to complete and is 65% hands-on. Classes meet in the Institute's 24 track studio and take advantage of the school's synthesizer programming room and audio/video reference library.

The program's curriculum is splint into three levels and includes classes in Recording Theory, Applied Music, Basic Electronics, Video Theory and Production, Studio Maintenance, Audio Sweetening, MIDI, Sound Effects, Sound Reinforcement, and Computer Programming, as well as labs and workshop.

Internships for students are arranged whenever possible.

School:	*Recording Institute of Detroit, Inc.*
Address:	*14611 E. 9 Mile Road* *East Detroit, MI 48021*
Phone:	*313-779-1380*
Program Director:	*Robert Dennis*
Admissions Director:	*Greg Kutcher*
Programs Offered:	*Recording Techniques*
Program Length:	*7-10 months*
Program Cost:	*$1,850*
Program Established:	*1976*
Accreditation:	*Michigan Department of Education*
Number of Studios:	*2*
Tracks per Studio:	*24*
Types of Recording:	*Analog, Digital*
Average Class Size:	*25 lecture, 12 lab*
Main Emphasis of Program:	*Hands-on training*

Additional Resources:
Financial Aid
Scholarships √
Professional Internships √
Job Placement √

Admission Policy:	*Open*
Admission Prerequisites:	*High school diploma or GED*

Classes Offered:

Analog Electronics		Digital Electronics	√
Physics	√	Acoustics	√
Music Theory	√	Music Performance	
Microphone Techniques	√	Pure Stereo Techniques	
Equipment Maintenance		Equipment Alignment	
Video Techniques		Film Techniques	
Business/ Marketing		Legal Aspects of Recording	
Electronic Music Synthesis		Computer/ MIDI Techniques	√
Sound Reinforcement		Audio System Design	

Profile:

The Recording Institute of Detroit's approach is to offer a training program that takes a person with no knowledge of the field to the skill level of being able to operate a fully equipped recording studio as an engineer. They then intern the student as an assistant engineer. If the graduate gets an entry level position in the field, he or she has the educational base necessary for quick advancement as the opportunities to do so present themselves.

The school is also aware that many people are planning activities in recording as a second career or as a hobby. Taking the Institute's first two courses sets up the graduate to be effective in home and demo recording used by hobbyists and songwriters.

Students interested in professional audio recording often first take the Basic Recording Course. This course gives the student techniques for obtaining good basic multitrack recordings and mixes. Students more interested in music and song writing often first take the Applied Music Theory Course. Recording students will take this as their second course. Students seeking a full time career in Music and Recording often go on to the Advanced Recording Course. This course is designed to give the student exposure to all the recording equipment normally used in a professional multitrack studio and to teach them to modify basic recording and mixing techniques for particular recording projects. The last step in the program is a 100 hour internship. Students act as an assistant in actual working circumstances, allowing them exposure to actual problems and their solutions by professionals.

To assist persons entering the field, the school offers a free career planning service to prospective students. The career planning results in recommendations that include the basic approaches and additional extra curricular activities designed to enhance the career potential of the applicant. After graduation from the Institute's program, the school offers intern placement and job placement assistance.

School:	*The Recording Workshop*
Address:	*455 Massieville Road* *Chillicothe, OH 45601*
Phone:	*614-663-2510 or 800-848-9900*
Program Director:	*Jim Rosebrook*
Admissions Director:	*Nancy Cottrill*
Programs Offered:	*Basic and Advanced Recording Engineering,* *Studio Maintenance and Trouble Shooting*
Program Length:	*1-5 weeks*
Program Cost:	*$395-$2,175*
Program Established:	*1972*
Accreditation:	*Ohio Department of Education*
Number of Studios:	*6*
Tracks per Studio:	*8, 16, 24*
Types of Recording:	*Analog, Digital*
Average Class Size:	*4 - 6*
Main Emphasis of Program:	*Operation of recording equipment*

Additional Resources:
Financial Aid
Scholarships
Professional Internships   √
Job Placement   √

Admission Policy:	*Selective*
Admission Prerequisites:	*None*

Classes Offered:

Analog Electronics	√	Digital Electronics	√
Physics	√	Acoustics	√
Music Theory	√	Music Performance	
Microphone Techniques	√	Pure Stereo Techniques	√
Equipment Maintenance	√	Equipment Alignment	√
Video Techniques		Film Techniques	
Business/ Marketing	√	Legal Aspects of Recording	√
Electronic Music Synthesis	√	Computer/ MIDI Techniques	√
Sound Reinforcement	√	Audio System Design	√

Profile:

The Recording Workshop, whose six studio complex is presently the largest educational facility of its kind in the United States, offers several courses of study. Their main program is a five week, 200 hour Recording Engineering and Music Production program, featuring a hands-on approach to learning the recording arts. From their 8 track media production studio with audio layback to video and SMPTE time code, to their 16 track studio with complete MIDI setup, to their fully automated 24 track studios, students work with equipment typically found in the recording industry. The school's curriculum covers all aspects of audio engineering, including in-studio music recording, commercial production, and mixing, as well as basic skills, such as editing, soldering, and tape machine alignment.

The Recording Workshop provides the opportunity for the student wanting the most education and experience in the shortest amount of time. From the very beginning, students are at the controls operating the equipment. The short term nature of this intensive five week program is especially appealing to those who cannot take more time out of their busy schedules. Using the skills and knowledge gained at The Workshop, graduates continue to refine their craft on the job, with as much potential for success as their dedication allows. This apprenticeship method has a time proven history of effectiveness in the recording industry.

Through their dedication to quality education, The Recording Workshop has become well established as an industry leader. Successful Workshop graduates are working throughout the world in major studios and with major artists.

No previous experience is required to participate in Workshop training. Classes are conveniently offered seven time annually, and on campus housing is available.

School:	***Red Wing Technical Institute***
Address:	*Highway 58*
	Red Wing, MN 55066
Phone:	*612-388-8271*
Program Director:	*Ed Dunn*
Admissions Director:	*Chuck Munson*
Programs Offered:	*Electronic Music Technology*
Program Length:	*18 months*
Program Cost:	*$2,800 Minnesota residents,*
	$5,600 non-residents
Program Established:	*1976*
Accreditation:	*Minnesota Department of Technical*
	Education
Number of Studios:	*2 shops*
Tracks per Studio:	*Not applicable*
Types of Recording:	*Not applicable*
Average Class Size:	*16*
Main Emphasis of Program:	*Electronic keyboard/music equipment*
	repair

Additional Resources:
Financial Aid √
Scholarships √
Professional Internships
Job Placement √

Admission Policy:	*Open*
Admission Prerequisites:	*High school diploma or GED*

Classes Offered:

Analog Electronics	√	Digital Electronics	√
Physics		Acoustics	√
Music Theory	√	Music Performance	
Microphone Techniques		Pure Stereo Techniques	
Equipment Maintenance	√	Equipment Alignment	√
Video Techniques		Film Techniques	
Business/ Marketing	√	Legal Aspects of Recording	
Electronic Music Synthesis	√	Computer/ MIDI Techniques	√
Sound Reinforcement		Audio System Design	

Profile:

The Electronic Music Technology program at the Red Wing Technical Institute is open to anyone with an interest in electronics. A background in music or computers is not necessary for entering into the course, but students will soon find themselves working their way through basic music and computer theory.

Preparing an electronic music technician at Red Wing is a process. It starts with basic electronic orientation and works through solid state and digital devices, integrated systems, memory and microprocessor controls, MIDI communication and computer Interface, and control of music and sound processing systems. A considerable amount of the 18 month program is devoted to practical " hands-on " application of the theory.

Graduates of the Electronic Music Technology program will be able to service and maintain all types of electronic music devices. They will also find a waiting job market. From employment as a factory representative of a major manufacturer to a one-person repair shop, the Electronic Music Technician is very much in demand.

Red Wing is nestled among the bluffs of the beautiful Hiawatha land along the Mississippi, just a short one hour drive from Minneapolis-St. Paul. A small community and a small school lend a personal touch to students as they live, work, and attend to the business of starting a new career. Red Wing also offers programs in Band Instrument Repair and Acoustical String Instrument Repair.

School:	**San Jose State University**
Address:	Electro-Acoustic Studios One Washington Square San Jose, CA 95192-0095
Phone:	408-924-4646/4673
Program Director:	Allen Strange
Admissions Director:	Allen Strange
Programs Offered:	B.A./B.M./M.A. with Specialization in Electro-Acoustics
Program Length:	4 years
Program Cost:	$50/semester California residents
Program Established:	
Accreditation:	NASM
Number of Studios:	4
Tracks per Studio:	4, 8, 16
Types of Recording:	Analog, Digital
Average Class Size:	10-18
Main Emphasis of Program:	Electronic music and recording arts
Additional Resources:	
Financial Aid	√
Scholarships	√
Professional Internships	
Job Placement	
Admission Policy:	Open
Admission Prerequisites:	Qualification as a music major in composition, performance or theory

Classes Offered:

Analog Electronics	√	Digital Electronics	√
Physics		Acoustics	√
Music Theory	√	Music Performance	√
Microphone Techniques	√	Pure Stereo Techniques	
Equipment Maintenance		Equipment Alignment	
Video Techniques		Film Techniques	√
Business/ Marketing		Legal Aspects of Recording	
Electronic Music Synthesis	√	Computer/ MIDI Techniques	√
Sound Reinforcement		Audio System Design	

Profile:

The Electro-Acoustic program at San Jose State University includes classes in keyboard synthesis, multitrack recording, studio synthesis, composition, performance, and computer aided instruction. additional courses in composition, studio production, and film scoring are available through the Jazz Studies program.

The Electro-Acoustics Studio currently accommodates two parallel courses in electronic music; Electro-Acoustic Concepts in Music and Advanced Electronic Music. Electro-Acoustic Concepts is an entry level class that provides an in depth study of analog synthesis techniques. Advanced Electronic Music addresses more individual composition/performance problems in electronic media and serves as an introduction to digital applications in electronic music. The hardware is a LSI-11 based system supporting virtually any language. The in-house language, MASC, is written in FIG-FORTH and currently accommodates 32 channels of DAC and ADC.

The studio instrumentation consists of a quad monitoring system, a Buchla 200/300 Electric Music Box, a Buchla Music Easel, a Buchla 100 Series System, and ancillary instruments consisting of Oberhiem, Arp, Moog, and EMS keyboard synthesizers, a Bode Vocoder, quad and stereo recording/playback and dubbing facilities, a Ohio Scientific Instruments 6502 Superboard Microprocessor, and a Terak 8510 Minicomputer for digital control of the analog instrumentation.

School:	*Sonoma State University*
Address:	*Department of Music* *School of Arts & Humanities* *Rohnert Park, CA 94928*
Phone:	*707-664-2324*
Program Director:	*Warren Dennis, Ron Pellegrino*
Admissions Director:	*Arthur Hills*
Programs Offered:	*Recording I-III, Studio Performance &* *Production, Music & Video, Sound Synthesis*
Program Length:	*1 semester per program*
Program Cost:	*$411/semester California residents,* *$411 + $156/unit non-residents*
Program Established:	*1981*
Accreditation:	*NASM*
Number of Studios:	*1*
Tracks per Studio:	*8*
Types of Recording:	*Analog, Digital, Video*
Average Class Size:	*12-15*
Main Emphasis of Program:	*Hands-on use by students*

Additional Resources:

Financial Aid	√
Scholarships	√
Professional Internships	√
Job Placement	

Admission Policy:	*Open*
Admission Prerequisites:	*Strong interest in recording, regular* *admission standards for California State* *University system*

Classes Offered:

Analog Electronics	√	Digital Electronics	
Physics	√	Acoustics	
Music Theory	√	Music Performance	√
Microphone Techniques	√	Pure Stereo Techniques	
Equipment Maintenance		Equipment Alignment	√
Video Techniques	√	Film Techniques	
Business/ Marketing		Legal Aspects of Recording	√
Electronic Music Synthesis	√	Computer/ MIDI Techniques	√
Sound Reinforcement	√	Audio System Design	

Profile:

Sonoma State University offers these programs through the Music Department of a Liberal Arts University. The complete range of traditional courses in music, physics, communications, and business are therefore available to the student enrolled In the technological specialties.

The recording program includes work in the fundamentals of studio recording and in the use of major types of recording equipment. The program is designed around a thorough hands on approach to the development of sound engineering skills, with an emphasis on the design and completion of a variety of recording projects. Advanced work is offered to develop skills in obtaining specific types of recorded sounds and in solving specific recording problems.

The sound synthesis program is similarly focused on a hands on approach to the principles and techniques of electric sound generation, modification, and control using digital and analog instruments. This program emphasizes performance and composition with current computer/synthesizer resources.

School: *Sound Investment Enterprises*

Address: *P.O.Box 4139*
Thousand Oaks, CA 91359

Phone: *805-499-0539*

Program Director: *Jim McCandliss*

Admissions Director: *Jim McCandliss*

Programs Offered: *Sound Workshop I, Sound Workshop II*

Program Length: *1-2 days*

Program Cost: *$90-$100*

Program Established: *1975*

Accreditation:

Number of Studios: *Not applicable*

Tracks per Studio: *Not applicable*

Types of Recording: *Analog*

Average Class Size: *40*

Main Emphasis of Program: *Live sound reproduction and reinforcement*

Additional Resources:
Financial Aid
Scholarships
Professional Internships
Job Placement

Admission Policy: *Open*

Admission Prerequisites: *None*

Classes Offered:

Analog Electronics		Digital Electronics	√
Physics		Acoustics	
Music Theory		Music Performance	
Microphone Techniques	√	Pure Stereo Techniques	
Equipment Maintenance		Equipment Alignment	
Video Techniques		Film Techniques	
Business/ Marketing		Legal Aspects of Recording	
Electronic Music Synthesis		Computer/ MIDI Techniques	
Sound Reinforcement	√	Audio System Design	√

Profile:

Sound Investment Enterprises offers one day Sound Shop workshops that are designed to guide the non-technician through the basics of audio equipment and its various applications in sound reinforcement systems. The workshops do not require a background in electronics or engineering.

Some of the topics cover: Microphone Selection and Use, Feedback Control, Wireless Microphone Systems, Mixing Guidelines, Cable and Connector Wiring, Portable and Permanent Sound Systems, Amplifiers and Speakers, Cassette Recording and Duplication, Sound Systems Vocabulary, and Monitor Systems.

Participants in the workshops also receive the program's Sound System Handbook, Volume I, for additional reference and troubleshooting.

Please contact Sound Investment Enterprises for more information about dates and locations of future Sound Shop workshops.

School:	*Sound Master Recording Schools*
Address:	*10747 Magnolia Blvd.*
	N. Hollywood, CA 91601
Phone:	*213-650-8000*
Program Director:	*Brian Ingoldsby*
Admissions Director:	*Barbara Ingoldsby*
Programs Offered:	*Recording Engineering, Video Production, Maintenance, Disc Mastering, Live Sound Reinforcement, and Remote Recording*
Program Length:	*1 year*
Program Cost:	*$2,500-$4,000*
Program Established:	*1974*
Accreditation:	*CSDE*
Number of Studios:	*3*
Tracks per Studio:	*16, 24, 40*
Types of Recording:	*Analog, Digital, Video*
Average Class Size:	*30 lecture, 10 lab*
Main Emphasis of Program:	*To produce viable personnel for the recording and video industry*
Additional Resources:	
Financial Aid	√
Scholarships	√
Professional Internships	√
Job Placement	√
Admission Policy:	*Selective*
Admission Prerequisites:	*High school diploma or GED*

Classes Offered:

Analog Electronics	√	Digital Electronics	√
Physics		Acoustics	√
Music Theory		Music Performance	
Microphone Techniques	√	Pure Stereo Techniques	
Equipment Maintenance	√	Equipment Alignment	√
Video Techniques	√	Film Techniques	
Business/ Marketing		Legal Aspects of Recording	
Electronic Music Synthesis		Computer/ MIDI Techniques	√
Sound Reinforcement	√	Audio System Design	

Profile:

Sound Master Recording Engineering School offers several programs in audio and video production, including Disc Mastering, Recording Studio Maintenance, Concert Sound Reinforcement, and four programs in multitrack Recording Engineering. Video production programs include a sequence of five Video Theory and Workshop programs, plus the unique Scuba Video program.

The Recording Engineering programs sequentially provide the theory, techniques, and knowledge of equipment required by the student wishing to become a professional audio engineer. The Disc Mastering program covers the basic principles of disc recording and provides the student with hands-on training in the operation of professional lathe systems. The Maintenance Engineering program covers everything from basic electronics through design and troubleshooting of studio equipment to general repair and maintenance of audio equipment. The Concert Sound Reinforcement program covers acoustic theory, speaker maintenance, and practical application of concert sound mixing.

The Video Production programs cover lighting, cameras, ENG and EFP, editing, directing, script writing, and producing. The Scuba Video program provides instruction in underwater videography. Participants must be certified scuba divers.

All of the Sound Master classes are conducted at the Sound Master Recording Studios and Color Video Production Center. The recording studio is equipped with 48 track automated recording consoles. The color video production center is complete with a sound stage, lighting, and state of the art cameras and editing systems. Also available are fully equipped five ton, mobile video trucks for location shoots, 24 track remote recording, and live sound reinforcement.

Graduates are given extensive job placement assistance, and the school has a continuous 88% job placement rate. Classes begin in September and March. The Sound Master Recording and Video Seminar is regularly held to describe the school's programs and to give basic demonstrations of the school's equipment to prospective students.

School:	*South Plains College*
Address:	*1400 College Avenue*
	Levelland, TX 79336
Phone:	*806-9611 ext. 271 or 279*
Program Director:	*Randy Ellis/Pat McCutchin*
Admissions Director:	*Randy Ellis/Pat McCutchin*
Programs Offered:	*Sound Technology, Performing Arts Production, A.A.S.*
Program Length:	*2 years*
Program Cost:	*$10/credit hour Texas residents, non-resident rates vary.*
Program Established:	*1980*
Accreditation:	*SASC, Texas Education Agency*
Number of Studios:	*5*
Tracks per Studio:	*4, 8, 16, 24*
Types of Recording:	*Analog, Digital, Video*
Average Class Size:	*10-20*
Main Emphasis of Program:	*Multitrack recording, sound reinforcement*

Additional Resources:
Financial Aid √
Scholarships √
Professional Internships
Job Placement

Admission Policy:	*Open*
Admission Prerequisites:	*High school diploma, ACT or CEEB*

Classes Offered:

Analog Electronics	√	Digital Electronics	√
Physics	√	Acoustics	√
Music Theory	√	Music Performance	√
Microphone Techniques	√	Pure Stereo Techniques	
Equipment Maintenance	√	Equipment Alignment	√
Video Techniques	√	Film Techniques	
Business/ Marketing	√	Legal Aspects of Recording	√
Electronic Music Synthesis	√	Computer/ MIDI Techniques	√
Sound Reinforcement	√	Audio System Design	√

Profile:

South Plains College has pioneered audio/video training efforts in the Southwest. In addition to their Sound Technology program, the college now offers a unique new program in Performing Arts Production Technology. Both programs are based on a 2-year course of study ending with an Associate of Applied Science degree in either Sound Technology or Performing Arts Production Technology.

Students receive most of their hands-on training through the use of two 4 track, one 8 track, and two 24 track recording studios. Also available for student use is a computer operated music synthesis lab. The cornerstone of both programs is the Tom T. Hall Recording and Production Studio, a $500,000 multi-use production center featuring a live sound stage, a complete video control room, a professional lighting system, and an automated 24 track audio recording facility.

Courses in the South Plains College Sound Technology program are designed to provide both the theory and practical experience necessary for employment as an audio engineer. The curriculum consists of 70 college hours of study and training in such specialized areas as multitrack recording and production, studio electronics, sound reinforcement, electronic music synthesis, and video production. additional classes in editing and duplication, music business careers, music, and performing arts production are also required. Students are provided hands-on experience through numerous music and recording projects in five professional caliber studios.

South Plains College is the only community college in Texas to offer a two year associates degree in Performing Arts Production Technology. This specialized program deals with all aspects of public entertainment events except the performers themselves. The curriculum consists of 65 college hours of training in such areas as television, audio production, sound reinforcement, stagecraft, and lighting. Hands-on training involves production of music videos, commercials, musical shows, dinner theaters, and fashion shows.

School:	*Southern Ohio College*
Address:	*Audio/Video Production*
	1055 Laidlaw Avenue
	Cincinnati, OH 45237
Phone:	*512-242-3791*
Program Director:	*Mark Turner*
Admissions Director:	*John Brown*
Programs Offered:	*Audio/Video Production*
Program Length:	*1-2 years*
Program Cost:	*$1,300 per semester*
Program Established:	*1982*
Accreditation:	*NCACS and AICS*
Number of Studios:	*4*
Tracks per Studio:	*2, 4, 16*
Types of Recording:	*Analog, Video*
Average Class Size:	*20*
Main Emphasis of Program:	*Corporate/industrial audio and video production*
Additional Resources:	
Financial Aid	√
Scholarships	√
Professional Internships	√
Job Placement	√
Admission Policy:	*Open*
Admission Prerequisites:	*High school diploma or GED*

Classes Offered:

Analog Electronics	√	Digital Electronics	
Physics		Acoustics	√
Music Theory		Music Performance	
Microphone Techniques	√	Pure Stereo Techniques	
Equipment Maintenance		Equipment Alignment	
Video Techniques	√	Film Techniques	
Business/ Marketing	√	Legal Aspects of Recording	√
Electronic Music Synthesis		Computer/ MIDI Techniques	
Sound Reinforcement		Audio System Design	√

Profile:

The Associate Degree program in Audio/Video Production at Southern Ohio College provides the graduate with the skills necessary to enter the expanding fields of business, industrial, and commercial communications. The curriculum encompasses general education, industry related business courses and specialized course that give the graduate practical knowledge in all aspects of audio and video production, including multitrack recording, audio for video sweetening, SMPTE time code, A/B roll video editing, and computerized graphics.

Students learn in a hands-on environment on state of the industry equipment. Audio facilities include two 2 track studios, a 4 track studio, and a 16 track studio which is set up with a full array of outboard gear, SMPTE time code, and a true chase system which allows audio sweetening for video.

The video facilities include two jump cut editing bays with SMPTE time code and an A/B roll editing bay with SMPTE time code, full list management, switcher interface, digital effects, and a computerized paint and graphics system. In addition to a 36' x 24' studio, there are two complete portable field production packages.

While some graduates find jobs in the broadcast industry, most decide to work in industrial and corporate communications and for major production facilities in the Cincinnati area.

Southern Ohio College is accredited by the North Central Association of Colleges and Schools and the Association of Independent Colleges and Schools.

School:	*Syracuse University*
Address:	*Newhouse School of Public Communications*
	Television-Radio-Film Department
	Syracuse, NY 13244
Phone:	*315-443-4004*
Program Director:	*Dr. Lawrence Meyers*
Admissions Director:	*Contact S.U. admissions office*
Programs Offered:	*B.S. and M.S. in Electronic Media Production*
Program Length:	*B.S.-4 years, M.S.-1 year*
Program Cost:	*$9,600 per year*
Program Established:	*1974*
Accreditation:	*Accrediting Council for Education in Journalism and Mass Communications*
Number of Studios:	*8*
Tracks per Studio:	*2, 4, 8, 16*
Types of Recording:	*Analog, Video, Film*
Average Class Size:	*16*
Main Emphasis of Program:	*Production techniques for television, radio, video, and film*
Additional Resources:	
Financial Aid	√
Scholarships	√
Professional Internships	√
Job Placement	√
Admission Policy:	*Highly selective*
Admission Prerequisites:	*Standard Syracuse University admission requirements*

Classes Offered:

Analog Electronics	√	Digital Electronics	√
Physics	√	Acoustics	√
Music Theory	√	Music Performance	√
Microphone Techniques	√	Pure Stereo Techniques	√
Equipment Maintenance	√	Equipment Alignment	√
Video Techniques	√	Film Techniques	√
Business/ Marketing	√	Legal Aspects of Recording	√
Electronic Music Synthesis	√	Computer/ MIDI Techniques	√
Sound Reinforcement		Audio System Design	√

Profile:

The Newhouse School of Communications at Syracuse University offers undergraduate and graduate degrees in Electronic Media Production. These programs prepare students to work in electronic media as producers, designers, and directors of audio/video productions. Though there is no specific degree program in audio, it is still possible to "major" in audio by taking advantage of flexible degree requirements and good advising. Students can take advantage of a wide variety of classes offered in the School of Communications, the School of Music and Art Media Studies Department in the College of Visual and Performing Arts, and the School of Engineering, as well as other University departments.

The Newhouse School and the Art Media Studies department both offer courses in audio, video, and film. The Newhouse School also offers other classes related to commercial radio and television production, electronic news gathering, and broadcast journalism. Students are able to take advantage of several audio and video production studios within the Newhouse School, as well as employment opportunities at three campus radio stations and with the Event Productions audio group that provides production support for campus concerts and shows.

Classes in music theory, music performance, electronic music composition, and music industry, as well as others, are offered through the School of Music. The Music School's facilities include a Roland MIDI Piano Lab, a CAI Music Theory and Ear Training Lab and an extensive electronic music studio, complete with a Macintosh based, multi-synth, MIDI system, a modular analog system, and 8 track recording facilities.

School:	*Tidewater Community College*
Address:	*1700 College Cresent* *Virginia Beach, VA 23456*
Phone:	*804-427-7294*
Program Director:	*Sam Ebersole*
Admissions Director:	*Sam Ebersole*
Programs Offered:	*A.A.S. in Radio/TV, Certificate in Media Production Techniques*
Program Length:	*1-2 years*
Program Cost:	*$17 per credit hour*
Program Established:	*1982*
Accreditation:	*SACS*
Number of Studios:	*1*
Tracks per Studio:	*4*
Types of Recording:	*Analog, Video*
Average Class Size:	*15*
Main Emphasis of Program:	*Video production*
Additional Resources:	
Financial Aid	√
Scholarships	
Professional Internships	√
Job Placement	
Admission Policy:	*Open*
Admission Prerequisites:	*High school diploma or GED*

Classes Offered:

Analog Electronics

Physics

Music Theory

Microphone Techniques √

Equipment Maintenance √

Video Techniques √

Business/ Marketing

Electronic Music Synthesis

Sound Reinforcement

Digital Electronics

Acoustics

Music Performance

Pure Stereo Techniques

Equipment Alignment

Film Techniques

Legal Aspects of Recording

Computer/ MIDI Techniques

Audio System Design

Profile:

Tidewater Community College offers a one year certificate in Media Production Technology and a two year Associate in Applied Science Degree in Graphic Communication. With new facilities for audio and video production, both in the field and the studio, the school provides a hands-on approach to learning. Students have an opportunity to produce audio and video productions utilizing current technologies in ENG/EFP and studio video production equipment. They also offer super-8mm film courses for those students interested in film.

Combining creativity with technical skills, courses in the curriculum range from TV Studio Art to Theory of Broadcast Equipment. Theory classes in News, Broadcast Management, and TV are taught by professionals in the Tidewater broadcast market. Interns have also been placed with local radio, TV, and other media related businesses.

School:	*Trebas Institute of Recording Arts*
Address:	*6602 Sunset Blvd.*
	Hollywood, CA 90028
	(see profile for other campuses)
Phone:	*213-467-6800*
Program Director:	*David P. Leonard, Executive Director*
Admissions Director:	*Denise Coyle*
Programs Offered:	*Recorded Music Production, Music Technology, Audio Engineering, Music Business Management*
Program Length:	*16 months*
Program Cost:	*Variable depending on campus and program*
Program Established:	*1979*
Accreditation:	*ACCET*
Number of Studios:	*2 per campus*
Tracks per Studio:	*8, 16, 24*
Types of Recording:	*Analog, Digital, Video*
Average Class Size:	*25 lecture, 8 lab*
Main Emphasis of Program:	*Recording arts and sciences with specialization in music business and music technology*
Additional Resources:	
Financial Aid	√
Scholarships	√
Professional Internships	√
Job Placement	√
Admission Policy:	*Selective*
Admission Prerequisites:	*High school diploma, musical or audio experience, creative portfolio*

Classes Offered:

Analog Electronics	√	Digital Electronics	√
Physics	√	Acoustics	√
Music Theory	√	Music Performance	√
Microphone Techniques	√	Pure Stereo Techniques	√
Equipment Maintenance	√	Equipment Alignment	√
Video Techniques	√	Film Techniques	√
Business/ Marketing	√	Legal Aspects of Recording	√
Electronic Music Synthesis	√	Computer/ MIDI Techniques	√
Sound Reinforcement	√	Audio System Design	√

Profile:

Vancouver Campus	*Toronto Campus*	*Ottawa Campus*	*Montreal Campus*
112 East 3rd Avenue	*410 Dundas St. E.*	*290 Nepean Street*	*1435 Bleury,#301*
Vancouver, BC	*Toronto, Ontario*	*Ottawa, Ontario*	*Montreal, Quebec*
CANADA V5T 1C8	*CANADA M5A 2A8*	*CANADA K1R 5G3*	*CANADA H3A 2H7*
ph:604-872-2666	*ph:416-966-3066*	*ph:613-232-7104*	*ph:514-845-4141*
Anne Arthur	*Kerry Keeler*	*James Henderson*	*Jacques Michaud*

Trebas Institute of Recording Arts was founded in 1979 by David P. Leonard with the goal of providing comprehensive college level training and education in the music business and the related audio/video recording arts and sciences. The objective is to give students the knowledge, practical skills, and professionalism required to function successfully in the music, film, television, and video industries in the decade ahead.

Trebas is international accredited by the Accrediting Commission of ACCET. TRABAS offers transfer credits between all of its campuses across North America. Several scholarships, up to $5,000 are available at each campus. Government loans and grants are also available to qualified students. Limited internships are available, and job placement assistance is provided. Foreign students are welcomed.

An academic staff of 75 instructors teach courses at Trebas. In 1988, a professional team of curriculum specialists revamped the entire Trebas Recording Arts & Sciences program to meet the future needs of the industry as expressed by many of its leaders in personal interviews.

Because recording technology is constantly changing, it has been the approach of Trebas, in additional to the hands on method, to teach basic concepts that will remain with graduates and be useful to them as long as they work in the industry. Trebas believes that just teaching equipment operations only results in "robots", and that is not their approach. Trebas promotes a comprehensive education in music technology, music business, and general communication skills.

School:	*UCLA Extension*
Address:	*10995 Le Conte Avnue, #437* *Los Angeles, CA 90024*
Phone:	*213-825-9064*
Program Director:	*Charles Swartz*
Admissions Director:	*Helen De Witty*
Programs Offered:	*Professional Designation in Recording Engineering*
Program Length:	*2 years*
Program Cost:	*$3,000-$4,000*
Program Established:	*1979*
Accreditation:	
Number of Studios:	*Rental studios used*
Tracks per Studio:	*24*
Types of Recording:	*Analog, Digital, Video, Film*
Average Class Size:	*20-40 lecture, 6-10 lab*
Main Emphasis of Program:	*Recording engineering*

Additional Resources:
Financial Aid √
Scholarships √
Professional Internships √
Job Placement

Admission Policy:	*Open*
Admission Prerequisites:	*Intermediate algebra, precalculus, basic physics, basic electronics*

Classes Offered:

Analog Electronics	√	Digital Electronics	√
Physics	√	Acoustics	√
Music Theory	√	Music Performance	√
Microphone Techniques	√	Pure Stereo Techniques	√
Equipment Maintenance	√	Equipment Alignment	√
Video Techniques	√	Film Techniques	√
Business/ Marketing	√	Legal Aspects of Recording	√
Electronic Music Synthesis	√	Computer/ MIDI Techniques	√
Sound Reinforcement	√	Audio System Design	√

Profile:

The Professional Designation in Recording Engineering is a rigorous training program that prepares the student in the art and science of recording engineering for all forms of recorded music in use today. The program utilizes state-of-the-art facilities and is instructed by top professionals from the recording industry.

Drawing on the talent and studio facilities in Los Angeles, one of the music industry capitals of the world, UCLA Extension has created a sequential curriculum of required and elective courses offering both theory and practice in audio technology and equipment, musicianship, and business practices. The objective is to enable the future engineer to acquire vision and problem solving techniques that meet the challenge of rapidly evolving technology and the sound recording market.

School:	*University of California-Santa Cruz*
Address:	*133 Communication Building*
	Santa Cruz, CA 95064
Phone:	*408-429-2369*
Program Director:	*Peter Elsea*
Admissions Director:	*Peter Elsea*
Programs Offered:	*Electronic Music*
Program Length:	*5 quarter sequence within B.A. program*
Program Cost:	*$50/semester California residents*
Program Established:	*1972*
Accreditation:	*WASC*
Number of Studios:	*3*
Tracks per Studio:	*4, 8*
Types of Recording:	*Analog, Video, Film*
Average Class Size:	*59 lecture, 15 lab*
Main Emphasis of Program:	*Composition*
Additional Resources:	
Financial Aid	√
Scholarships	√
Professional Internships	√
Job Placement	
Admission Policy:	*Highly selective*
Admission Prerequisites:	*Standard University of California*
	requirements

Classes Offered:

Analog Electronics	√	Digital Electronics	√
Physics	√	Acoustics	√
Music Theory	√	Music Performance	√
Microphone Techniques	√	Pure Stereo Techniques	√
Equipment Maintenance		Equipment Alignment	
Video Techniques	√	Film Techniques	√
Business/ Marketing		Legal Aspects of Recording	
Electronic Music Synthesis	√	Computer/ MIDI Techniques	√
Sound Reinforcement	√	Audio System Design	

Profile:

Established as an alternative approach to university education, the philosophy of UCSC emphasizes attention to the individual needs of the student through such policies as a collegiate structure, small classes, and narrative evaluation for each course instead of grades.

The UCSC electronic music program provides training in emerging music technologies to students of any discipline, especially those in music, video, and computer engineering. Courses are taught by Gordon Mumma, who is one of the pioneers of the field and a respected composer, and by Peter Elsea, who combines a detailed technical knowledge with the ability to present such material in a readily comprehensible form. Other faculty who are active in electronic music or related research are Professors David Cope, Frederic Lieberman, David Jones, and Kevin Karplus.

The program consists of a two year sequence of courses: History, Technology, and Literature of electronic music, traditional electronic music techniques, computer assisted techniques, advanced composition, electronic skills for musicians, and workshops. The first course is a survey open to all students; the following courses are restricted to 15 students per section to ensure adequate studio access. The workshop is a forum for students to pursue individual music and research projects for as many quarters as they wish.

Recording skills are not taught in a separate course; rather they are developed in all of the courses as part of a full compliment of techniques required of the modern musician. The emphasis of the program is on developing creative ability in music composition and production, and on building fundamental skills that can be applied to the newest technology as it appears. The equipment chosen for the studios is representative of that which students can expect to find in post graduate life rather than expensive esoterica. Equipment is kept up to date and in excellent operating condition.

Standards are high; students are expected to produce work that is original in concept and at prevailing professional standards in execution. There are no stylistic restrictions on students' work, and each is allowed at least eight hours per week of studio time. Graduates have gone on to successful careers in all related fields, including advertising, record production, instrument manufacturing, and pro audio.

School:	*University of Colorado at Denver*
Address:	*College of Music*
	1200 Laramer Street
	Denver, CO 80204
Phone:	*303-556-2727*
Program Director:	*Bill Porter*
Admissions Director:	*Roy Pritts*
Programs Offered:	*B.S. in Music with Music Engineering emphasis*
Program Length:	*4 years*
Program Cost:	*$605/semster Colorado residents*
	$2,800/semester non-residents
Program Established:	*1974*
Accreditation:	*NASM*
Number of Studios:	*3*
Tracks per Studio:	*4, 8, 16*
Types of Recording:	*Analog, Video*
Average Class Size:	*30 lecture, 15 lab*
Main Emphasis of Program:	*Audio engineering*

Additional Resources:
Financial Aid √
Scholarships √
Professional Internships √
Job Placement √

Admission Policy:	*Selective*
Admission Prerequisites:	*High school diploma, entrance audition, ACT score of 21, GPA of 2.0 for transfers or freshman*

Classes Offered:

Analog Electronics	√	Digital Electronics	√
Physics		Acoustics	√
Music Theory	√	Music Performance	√
Microphone Techniques	√	Pure Stereo Techniques	√
Equipment Maintenance	√	Equipment Alignment	√
Video Techniques	√	Film Techniques	
Business/ Marketing	√	Legal Aspects of Recording	√
Electronic Music Synthesis	√	Computer/ MIDI Techniques	√
Sound Reinforcement	√	Audio System Design	√

Profile:

The Recording Technology and Sound Synthesis program at the University of Colorado at Denver enrolls students preparing for careers in the music industry. The program addresses the state of contemporary technology in studio recording, sound reinforcement, and electronic music, utilizing both analog and digital techniques. Studies in history, hardware, and techniques common to commercial applications, as well as lab and field work, are intended to develop skills within creative musicians, producers, and technicians. Professional internships are required, and the school's placement program for Music Engineering students has a 78% success rate. Graduates work with the Phoenix Symphony, the Record Plant in Los Angeles, Universal Recording in Chicago, SPARS, A & M Records, and United Cable Television, as well as new music-related businesses created by graduates themselves.

Facilities within the College of Music include a self-paced learning center, a computer music lab, an electronic music and synthesis lab, and a complex of recording studios for 4, 8, and 16-track recording. Students also have access to three fully equipped video studios that include synchronized audio facilities.

The School's faculty includes Roy Pritts, Bill Porter, and Martin Polon, all influential names in audio education. Acting Dean of the College of Music, Roy Pritts and Assistant Professor Martin Polon are both active with the Audio Engineering Society's Education Committee and are responsible for the AES Directory of Educational Programs. Bill Porter, the unofficial head of the Music Engineering department, has the destinction of being the first person inducted into Absolute Sound magazine's Audio Hall of Fame for lifetime achievement in recording, having engineered 300 charted records and 37 gold records for artists such as Elvis Presley and the Everly Brothers.

The College of Music is currently working on developing a Master of Science in Music degree with an emphsis in music technology and management.

School:	*University of Hartford*
Address:	*College of Engineering*
	West Hartford, CT 06117
Phone:	*203-243-4792*
Program Director:	*Robert Celmer*
Admissions Director:	*Robert Celmer*
Programs Offered:	*B.S. in Engineering: Acoustics and Music*
Program Length:	*4 years*
Program Cost:	*$8,830*
Program Established:	*1976*
Accreditation:	*State of Conneticut*
Number of Studios:	*3*
Tracks per Studio:	*4, 8, 16*
Types of Recording:	*Analog, Digital*
Average Class Size:	*10 music, 20 engineering*
Main Emphasis of Program:	*Engineering acoustics and usic*

Additional Resources:
Financial Aid √
Scholarships √
Professional Internships √
Job Placement √

Admission Policy:	*Selective*
Admission Prerequisites:	*Audition for Hartt School of Music, english, social studies, foreign language, chemistry and physics, algebra, geometry, and trigonometry*

Classes Offered:

Analog Electronics	√	Digital Electronics	√
Physics	√	Acoustics	√
Music Theory	√	Music Performance	√
Microphone Techniques	√	Pure Stereo Techniques	√
Equipment Maintenance		Equipment Alignment	
Video Techniques		Film Techniques	
Business/ Marketing		Legal Aspects of Recording	
Electronic Music Synthesis	√	Computer/ MIDI Techniques	√
Sound Reinforcement	√	Audio System Design	√

Profile:

The University of Hartford offers combined options in Acoustics and Music within the Interdisciplinary Engineering Studies Program at the College of Engineering. This unique, rigorous curriculum leads to the Bachelor of Science in Engineering degree. The program includes a basic engineering core as well as a major concentration in vibrations, acoustics, and courses offered by the Hartt School of Music.

The program is designed for students who have an aptitude and desire for a career involved in the application of modern technology to the field of music and/or acoustics. To be accepted into this unique curriculum applicants must have the math and science background required of all engineering students and must successfully pass the entrance requirements of the Hartt School, including a music audition.

Although the curriculum is scheduled to be completed within four years, it is certainly the most rigorous undergraduate program at the University, requiring a minimum of 142 credits for completion and often extending to 146 credits. The Acoustics and Music students, typically the school's brightest students, bring a special perspective to their studies because of their dual pursuits.

Graduates will have a personalized, career-oriented education with which to use engineering as a broad technical base for a challenging career in acoustics and/or music.

School:	*University of Lowell*
Address:	*College of Music* *Sound Recording Technology* *Lowell, MA 01854*
Phone:	*508-452-5000 ext. 2251*
Program Director:	*William Moylan*
Admissions Director:	*William Moylan*
Programs Offered:	*B.M. in Sound Recording Technology, Minors in SRT for E.E. and Computer Science majors*
Program Length:	*4 years-B.M., 2 years-Minor*
Program Cost:	*$1,400/year Massachusetts residents, $3,200/year non-residents*
Program Established:	*1983*
Accreditation:	*NASM*
Number of Studios:	*7*
Tracks per Studio:	*2, 4, 8, 24*
Types of Recording:	*Analog, Digital, Video*
Average Class Size:	*8 - 22*
Main Emphasis of Program:	*Music recording*

Additional Resources:

Financial Aid	√
Scholarships	√
Professional Internships	√
Job Placement	√

Admission Policy:	*Selective*
Admission Prerequisites:	*High school diploma, music audition, high GPA in math, music, and freshman courses*

Classes Offered:

Analog Electronics	√	Digital Electronics	√
Physics	√	Acoustics	√
Music Theory	√	Music Performance	√
Microphone Techniques	√	Pure Stereo Techniques	√
Equipment Maintenance	√	Equipment Alignment	√
Video Techniques	√	Film Techniques	
Business/ Marketing	√	Legal Aspects of Recording	√
Electronic Music Synthesis	√	Computer/ MIDI Techniques	√
Sound Reinforcement	√	Audio System Design	√

Profile:

The University of Lowell offers three degree programs in Sound Recording Technology: the Bachelor of Music degree in Sound Recording Technology, a Minor in SRT for Electrical Engineering majors, and a Minor in SRT for Computer Science majors. The programs are rigorous in their demands for quality performance from the student, but placement of graduates is nearly 100%.

The program has state of the art recording, mixing, sound reinforcement, video-post, and sound synthesis and MIDI studios, and equipment design and computer laboratories to support its 16 sound recording courses. The program has drawn from the wealth of high technology industry talent and the cultural and artistic communities found in the greater Boston area, to form a professional faculty of renowned technical and artistic experts .

The Bachelor of Music in Sound Recording Technology is offered through the College of Music. The goal of the program is to produce a musically sophisticated and sensitive professional with sufficient technical knowledge to excel in the present production industry and to easily keep pace with the changing technology. The program combines studies in physics, electrical engineering, computer science, math, and traditional studies in music with at least nine courses in the art and technology of recording. The degree culminates with the "Recording Industry" course where students explore career venues and prepare to undertake a required 15 week professional internship at a recording, television, radio, or video studio, motion picture sound stage, or other venue agreed upon between the Coordinator of the program and the student.

The Minor in SRT for Electrical Engineering majors is offered through the College of Music in conjunction with the College of Engineering and is designed to develop qualified individuals for careers in audio engineering R&D and technical maintenance. The program provides the student with practical knowledge of audio and video equipment, equipment maintenance, design theories and applications, theory of audio equipment operation, and basic music skills. The program culminates with a final research project.

The Minor is SRT for Computer Science majors is designed to develop qualified individuals for careers in audio related software development. The minor produces a technically accurate and knowledgeable individual who has an awareness of concerns and concepts of the artistic, functional, and technical aspects of the recording industry. The minor is offered by the College of Music in conjunction with Department of Computer Science in the College of Pure and Applied Sciences.

School:	*University of Miami*
Address:	*School of Music*
	Gusman Hall
	Coral Gables, FL 33124
Phone:	*305-284-2245*
Program Director:	*Ken Pohlmann*
Admissions Director:	*Jo Faulmann*
Programs Offered:	*B.M. in Music Engineering Technology, M.S. in Audio Engineering*
Program Length:	*B.M.-4 years, M.S.-2 years*
Program Cost:	*$285/credit hour, undergraduate*
	$435/credit hour, graduate
Program Established:	*1975*
Accreditation:	*NASM*
Number of Studios:	*2*
Tracks per Studio:	*24*
Types of Recording:	*Analog, Digital, Video*
Average Class Size:	*20*
Main Emphasis of Program:	*Audio engineering and recording*
Additional Resources:	
Financial Aid	√
Scholarships	√
Professional Internships	√
Job Placement	√
Admission Policy:	*Highly selective*
Admission Prerequisites:	*Music audition, SAT scores of 1200 recommended for B.M., B.S. in Electrical Engineering or B.M. in Music Engineering for M.S.*

Classes Offered:

Analog Electronics	√	Digital Electronics	√
Physics	√	Acoustics	√
Music Theory	√	Music Performance	√
Microphone Techniques	√	Pure Stereo Techniques	√
Equipment Maintenance	√	Equipment Alignment	√
Video Techniques	√	Film Techniques	√
Business/ Marketing	√	Legal Aspects of Recording	√
Electronic Music Synthesis	√	Computer/ MIDI Techniques	√
Sound Reinforcement	√	Audio System Design	√

Profile:

The Music Engineering program at the University of Miami was the first bachelor degree program in the U.S. to offer a curriculum balanced between music, audio, and electrical engineering. The program now offers both a four year Bachelor of Music Engineering degree with a minor in electrical engineering, as well as a two year Master of Science Audio Engineering degree.

Courses in the undergraduate curriculum included recording engineering, digital audio, acoustics and studio design, studio maintenance, video production, computer programming, circuit theory, music business, music theory, arranging, and music performance. All applicants to the program must pass a music performance audition and submit competitive SAT scores.

The Master's degree curriculum emphasizes electrical engineering graduate courses, as well as study in advanced digital audio, video, psychoacoustics, logic design, and a research thesis. The Master's degree program accepts students with undergraduate degrees in electrical engineering or graduates from the undergraduate Music Engineering program with its minor in electrical engineering.

Hands-on experience in the University's recording studio provides understanding of techniques and applications. The principle studio houses an automated Sony MXP-3036 console, MCI 2 and 24 track recorders, 3M and Mitsubishi digital recorders, dbx digital audio processor, Audio Kinetics synchronization system, Sony 3/4" video recorders, a Synclavier, and other equipment.

In its 16 year history, graduates from the Music Engineering program have recorded gold, platinum and Grammy-award winning albums. The program has attracted students from across the U.S. and from a dozen foreign countries. Thanks to industry acceptance, the program enjoys a 100% placement rate of its graduates.

School:	*University of Wiscosin-Oshkosh*
Address:	*Music Department* *800 Algoma Blvd.* *Oshkosh, WI 54901*
Phone:	*414-424-4224*
Program Director:	*Charles Isaacson*
Admissions Director:	*Charles Isaacson*
Programs Offered:	*Music Merchandising - Recording*
Program Length:	*4 years*
Program Cost:	*$3,600/year Wisconsin residents,* *$6,400/year non-residents*
Program Established:	*1982*
Accreditation:	*NASM*
Number of Studios:	*1*
Tracks per Studio:	*8, 16*
Types of Recording:	*Analog*
Average Class Size:	*20*
Main Emphasis of Program:	*Music Recording*
Additional Resources:	
Financial Aid	√
Scholarships	√
Professional Internships	√
Job Placement	
Admission Policy:	*Selective*
Admission Prerequisites:	*Music audition, regular University* *admission requirements*

Classes Offered:

Analog Electronics		Digital Electronics	
Physics		Acoustics	√
Music Theory	√	Music Performance	√
Microphone Techniques	√	Pure Stereo Techniques	√
Equipment Maintenance	√	Equipment Alignment	√
Video Techniques		Film Techniques	
Business/ Marketing	√	Legal Aspects of Recording	√
Electronic Music Synthesis		Computer/ MIDI Techniques	
Sound Reinforcement		Audio System Design	

Profile:

The Recording Technology emphasis is part of the Bachelor of Music in Music Merchandising Program at the University of Wisconsin-Oshkosh. It is a comprehensive major requiring a 52 credit core of music courses, including a senior recital, 19 credits in recording courses, 15 credits in business courses, and 44 credits in general education.

The recording sequence begins with two theory and principles courses. Subsequent courses provide the student with increasing hands-on experiences In the studlo. The sequence culminates in two semester long practicum courses where the student, under the guidance of the instructor, is responsible for entire recording projects from start to finish. Upon completion of all course work, the student does a 14 week internship at a recording studio.

The Recording Technology program's strengths are the hands-on learning opportunities provided, the studio facilities, and the challenge of meeting rigorous academic, musical, and technical standards.

School:	*Weaver Education Center*
Address:	*Greensboro Public Schools*
	300 S. Spring Street
	Greensboro, NC 27435
Phone:	*919-370-8282*
Program Director:	*Ronald Follas*
Admissions Director:	*Ronald Follas*
Programs Offered:	*Electronic Music, Audio Engineering*
Program Length:	*1 year per course*
Program Cost:	*None- open only to Greensboro high school students*
Program Established:	*1978*
Accreditation:	*SACS*
Number of Studios:	*5*
Tracks per Studio:	*4, 8*
Types of Recording:	*Analog*
Average Class Size:	*14*
Main Emphasis of Program:	*Synthesizer programming and composition*

Additional Resources:
Financial Aid
Scholarships
Professional Internships √
Job Placement

Admission Policy:	*Open*
Admission Prerequisites:	*Students must be currently enrolled juniors or seniors in one of the Greensboro high schools. Guilford county students may be admitted if room is available.*

Classes Offered:

Analog Electronics		Digital Electronics	
Physics		Acoustics	√
Music Theory	√	Music Performance	√
Microphone Techniques	√	Pure Stereo Techniques	√
Equipment Maintenance		Equipment Alignment	
Video Techniques		Film Techniques	√
Business/ Marketing		Legal Aspects of Recording	√
Electronic Music Synthesis	√	Computer/ MIDI Techniques	√
Sound Reinforcement	√	Audio System Design	√

Profile:

The Philip J. Weaver Education Center is a centrally located extension of the four public high schools in Greensboro, North Carolina. Courses offered are unique within the system, do not have sufficient enrollment at each high school, are too expensive at all sights, or conflict with the student's home school schedule. The curriculum includes vocational, performing and visual arts, and advanced academic programs. Among these programs are courses in Electronic Music and Audio Engineering.

Electronic Music I is open to all currently enrolled juniors and seniors in the Greensboro public schools and includes analog and digital synthesizer programming, basic recording techniques, composition, and other areas of interest to the students. Electronic Music II allows students a substantial amount of time in the composition studio as well as experience in recording, microphone placement techniques, and operation of the equipment in the audio engineering studio. Students form two bands which alternate as studio bands and audio engineers for practical experience in the recording studio.

Students from the Electronic Music program at the Weaver Education Center often continue their study at recording workshops, audio engineering schools, and university schools of music. Some former students from the Weaver Center are now studio musicians and audio engineers in Nashville, New York, and Los Angeles.

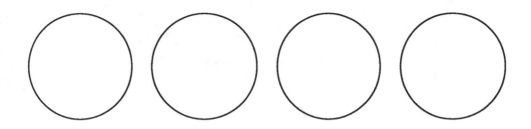

Additional
Programs

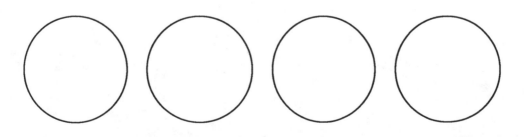

School:	*Goodnight Audio*
Address:	*11260 Goodnight Lane*
	Dallas, TX 75229
Phone:	*214-241-5182*
Program Director:	*Ruben Ayala*
Admissions Director:	*Ruben Ayala*
Programs Offered:	*Elementary and Advanced Recording*
Program Length:	*30 hours*
Program Cost:	*$500*
Program Established:	*1983*
Accreditation:	*None*
Number of Studios:	*1*
Tracks per Studio:	*24*
Types of Recording:	*Analog, Digital*
Average Class Size:	*5*
Main Emphasis of Program:	*Hands-on recording*

Additional Resources:
Financial Aid
Scholarships
Professional Internships
Job Placement

Admission Policy:	*Open*
Admission Prerequisites:	*None*

School:	*Institute of Audio/Video Engineering*
Address:	*1831 Hyperion Avenue* *Hollywood, CA 90027*
Phone:	*800-972-1414 or 800-551-8877*
Program Director:	*Ted Shreffler*
Admissions Director:	*Ted Shreffler*
Programs Offered:	*Recording Engineering*
Program Length:	*24 weeks*
Program Cost:	*$6,000*
Program Established:	*1980*
Accreditation:	*NATTS*
Number of Studios:	*4*
Tracks per Studio:	*2-24*
Types of Recording:	*Analog, Video*
Average Class Size:	*26 lecture, 8-12 labs*
Main Emphasis of Program:	*Audio recording knowledge and skills*

Additional Resources:
Financial Aid	√
Scholarships	
Professional Internships	√
Job Placement	√

Admission Policy:	*Open*
Admission Prerequisites:	*High school diploma or equivalent, personal interview*

School:	*JTM Workshop of Recording Arts*
Address:	*P.O. Box 606*
	Knox, PA 16232
Phone:	*814-797-5883*
Program Director:	*Frank Thomas Battista*
Admissions Director:	*Frank Thomas Battista*
Programs Offered:	*Audio Engineering*
Program Length:	*5 weeks*
Program Cost:	*$1,595*
Program Established:	*1984*
Accreditation:	*Pennsylvania Department of Education*
Number of Studios:	*2*
Tracks per Studio:	*2, 4, 8, 24*
Types of Recording:	*Analog*
Average Class Size:	*3 - 6*
Main Emphasis of Program:	*Audio engineering*

Additional Resources:
Financial Aid √
Scholarships
Professional Internships
Job Placement √

Admission Policy:	*Open*
Admission Prerequisites:	*Strong desire to learn recording engineering*

School:	*McGill University*
Address:	*Faculty of Music* *555 Sherbrooke* *Montreal, P.Q., H3A 1E3, CANADA*
Phone:	*514-398-4546*
Program Director:	*Wieslaw Woszczyk*
Admissions Director:	*Veronica Slobodian*
Programs Offered:	*M.M. in Sound Recording*
Program Length:	*2 years*
Program Cost:	*$900 Canadian citizens, $9,000 others*
Program Established:	*1979*
Accreditation:	
Number of Studios:	*3*
Tracks per Studio:	*2, 24*
Types of Recording:	*Analog, Digital*
Average Class Size:	*4 - 5*
Main Emphasis of Program:	*Music recording*
Additional Resources:	
Financial Aid	√
Scholarships	√
Professional Internships	
Job Placement	
Admission Policy:	*Highly selective*
Admission Prerequisites:	*Bachelor of Music degree, professional &* *artistic experience considered, non-McGill* *applicants must also complete a year of* *undergraduate prerequisites.*

School:	*Mixmaster Recording Engineering Schools*
Address:	*4877 Mercury Street*
	San Diego, CA 92111
Phone:	*619-569-7367*
Program Director:	*Garth Hedin*
Admissions Director:	*Garth Hedin*
Programs Offered:	*Beginning, Intermediate, Advanced Recording, SMPTE/MIDI/Computer, Video*
Program Length:	*6 weeks per course*
Program Cost:	*$300 per course*
Program Established:	*1985*
Accreditation:	*California Department of Education*
Number of Studios:	*5*
Tracks per Studio:	*8, 16, 24*
Types of Recording:	*Analog, Film*
Average Class Size:	*5*
Main Emphasis of Program:	*Hands-on training*

Additional Resources:
Financial Aid
Scholarships
Professional Internships √
Job Placement √

Admission Policy:	*Selective*
Admission Prerequisites:	*None*

School:	*Nickel Recording*
Address:	*Media Arts Center*
	168 Buckingham Street
	Hartford, CT 06106
Phone:	*203-524-5656*
Program Director:	*Jack Stang*
Admissions Director:	*Jack Stang*
Programs Offered:	*Recording Techniques 1 & 2*
	Record Production 1 & 2
Program Length:	*10 weeks per program*
Program Cost:	
Program Established:	*1975*
Accreditation:	*Hartford Conservatory*
Number of Studios:	*2*
Tracks per Studio:	*8, 24*
Types of Recording:	*Analog*
Average Class Size:	*15*
Main Emphasis of Program:	*Audio engineering*
Additional Resources:	
Financial Aid	
Scholarships	
Professional Internships	
Job Placement	
Admission Policy:	*Open*
Admission Prerequisites:	*None*

School:	*San Antonio College*
Address:	*Radio-TV-Film Department* *1300 San Pedro Avenue* *San Antonio, TX 78284*
Phone:	*512-733-2793*
Program Director:	*Fred Weiss*
Admissions Director:	*Donnie Meals*
Programs Offered:	*Techniques in Multitrack Recording*
Program Length:	*1 semester*
Program Cost:	*$100*
Program Established:	*1984*
Accreditation:	
Number of Studios:	*1*
Tracks per Studio:	*8*
Types of Recording:	*Analog*
Average Class Size:	*15*
Main Emphasis of Program:	*Advanced commercial production*

Additional Resources:

Financial Aid	√
Scholarships	
Professional Internships	√
Job Placement	

Admission Policy:	*Selective*
Admission Prerequisites:	*Previous basic audio experience, approval of instructor*

School:	*School of Audio Engineering*
Address:	*3000 South Robertson Blvd.* *Suite 100* *Los Angeles, California 90034*
Phone:	*213-559-0973*
Program Director:	*Iain P.Everinston*
Admissions Director:	*Cheryl A. Abott*
Programs Offered:	*Audio Engineering, Tonmeister*
Program Length:	*15 months*
Program Cost:	*$6,105*
Program Established:	*1979*
Accreditation:	*California State*
Number of Studios:	*3*
Tracks per Studio:	*8, 16, 24*
Types of Recording:	*Analog, Digital*
Average Class Size:	*25*
Main Emphasis of Program:	*Audio engineering*

Additional Resources:
Financial Aid √
Scholarships √
Professional Internships √
Job Placement √

Admission Policy:	*Open*
Admission Prerequisites:	*Entrance examination*

School:	*The School of the Ozarks*
Address:	*Mass Media Department*
	Pt. Lookout, MO 65726
Phone:	*417-334-6411*
Program Director:	*Bob Lake*
Admissions Director:	*Bob Lake*
Programs Offered:	*B.S./B.A. in Mass Media*
Program Length:	*4 years*
Program Cost:	*Free for work-study students*
Program Established:	*1983*
Accreditation:	*NCAC*
Number of Studios:	*2*
Tracks per Studio:	*8*
Types of Recording:	*Analog, Video*
Average Class Size:	*10-20*
Main Emphasis of Program:	*Media production*

Additional Resources:

Financial Aid	√
Scholarships	√
Professional Internships	√
Job Placement	√

Admission Policy:	*Highly selective*
Admission Prerequisites:	*High school diploma, ACT scores, physical exam, SAR/Pell forms, 2 letters of reference*

School:	*Select Sound Studios*
Address:	*2315 Elmwood Avenue*
	Kenmore, NY 14217
Phone:	*716-873-2717*
Program Director:	*Richard Bauerle*
Admissions Director:	*Chuck Mandrell*
Programs Offered:	*Workshop I, Workshop II, Workshop III*
Program Length:	*8-12 weeks per program*
Program Cost:	*$395 per program*
Program Established:	*1979*
Accreditation:	*Buffalo State College, Villa Maria College*
Number of Studios:	*2*
Tracks per Studio:	*16, 24*
Types of Recording:	*Analog, Video*
Average Class Size:	*12*
Main Emphasis of Program:	
Additional Resources:	
Financial Aid	
Scholarships	
Professional Internships	√
Job Placement	
Admission Policy:	*Open*
Admission Prerequisites:	*Strong interest in the professional audio business*

School:	*Sunset Productions*
Address:	*Recording Workshop*
	117 West 8th
	Hays, KS 67601
Phone:	*913-625-9634*
Program Director:	*Mark Meckel*
Admissions Director:	*Mark Meckel*
Programs Offered:	*Recording Workshop*
Program Length:	*1 week*
Program Cost:	*$500*
Program Established:	*1979*
Accreditation:	*Fort Hays State University*
Number of Studios:	*1*
Tracks per Studio:	*16*
Types of Recording:	*Analog, Digital*
Average Class Size:	*2*
Main Emphasis of Program:	*Hands-on experience for two students*

Additional Resources:
Financial Aid
Scholarships
Professional Internships
Job Placement

Admission Policy:	*Selective*
Admission Prerequisites:	*None*

School:	*University of Illinois at Urbana-Champaign*
Address:	*2136 Music Building*
	1114 W. Nevada
	Urbana, IL 61801
Phone:	*217-244-1207*
Program Director:	*James Beauchamp*
Admissions Director:	*James Beauchamp*
Programs Offered:	*B.S. in Electrical Engineering with Audio Emphasis*
Program Length:	*4 years*
Program Cost:	*$4,000/year Illinois residents, $6,000/year non-residents*
Program Established:	*1969*
Accreditation:	
Number of Studios:	*7*
Tracks per Studio:	*2 - 8*
Types of Recording:	*Analog, Digital*
Average Class Size:	*20*
Main Emphasis of Program:	*Theory and design of audio/electronic music systems*
Additional Resources:	
Financial Aid	√
Scholarships	√
Professional Internships	
Job Placement	
Admission Policy:	*Highly selective*
Admission Prerequisites:	*High school diploma, high GPA and SAT scores*

School:	*University of North Alabama*
Address:	*Box 5183*
	Florence AL 35632-0001
Phone:	*205-760-4361*
Program Director:	*James Simpson*
Admissions Director:	*James Simpson*
Programs Offered:	*B.A./B.S. in Commercial Music*
Program Length:	*4 years*
Program Cost:	*Standard University Tuition*
Program Established:	*1975*
Accreditation:	*NASM*
Number of Studios:	*Rental studios used*
Tracks per Studio:	*Depends on rental studio*
Types of Recording:	*Analog*
Average Class Size:	*20*
Main Emphasis of Program:	*Music business*

Additional Resources:
Financial Aid √
Scholarships √
Professional Internships √
Job Placement

Admission Policy:	*Open*
Admission Prerequisites:	*High school diploma or GED*

School:	*University of Sound Arts*
Address:	*1645 North Vine Street, Suite 350* *Hollywood, CA 90028*
Phone:	*213-467-5256*
Program Director:	*Jerry Bernstein*
Admissions Director:	*Jerry Bernstein*
Programs Offered:	*Audio/Video Engineering*
Program Length:	*9-18 months*
Program Cost:	*$7,980*
Program Established:	*1976*
Accreditation:	*ACCET*
Number of Studios:	*3*
Tracks per Studio:	*24*
Types of Recording:	*Analog, Digital, Video*
Average Class Size:	*8*
Main Emphasis of Program:	*Recording engineering*

Additional Resources:
Financial Aid √
Scholarships √
Professional Internships √
Job Placement √

Admission Policy:	*Highly selective*
Admission Prerequisites:	*High school diploma or GED, SAT*

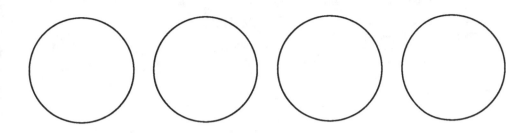

Master List
of
Audio Programs

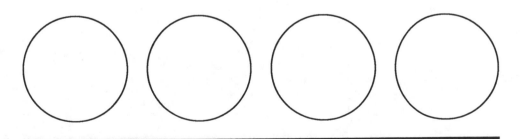

This master list contains names and addresses of over 300 audio schools and programs. When possible, a contact person and phone number has also been provided. Entries are listed alphabetically by state or country. Programs featured in New Ears are listed in bold.

ALABAMA

SRS Recording Studio
536 Huffman Rd.
Birmingham, AL.
Noel White

Studio Four
1918 Wise Drive
Dothan, AL 36303
Jerry Wise
205-794-9067

University of Alabama
Sound Cell Inc.
601 Meridian St.
Huntsville, AL 35801
Douglas Smith
205-539-1868

University of North Alabama
Box 5183
Florence, AL 35632
James Simpson
205-760-4361

Woodrich Studios
PO Box 38
Lexington, AL 35648
Woody Richardson
205-247-3983

ARIZONA

Academy of Recording Sciences
14447 N. 20th St.
Phoenix, AZ 85022
J. Vlcan
602-493-9898

Conservatory of Recording Arts & Sciences
14447 N. 20th St.
Phoenix, AZ
Mary Goodenow
602-493-9898

Gabriel's Arizona Remote Recorders
833 W. Main St.
Mesa, AZ 85201
Wayne Mitchell
602-834-9511

Pima Community College
2202 W. Anklam Rd.
Tucson, AZ 85709
David Wing
602-884-6974

SKE Publishing
PO Box 2519-M
Sedona, AZ 86336
Sean Kean
602-282-1258

University of Arizona
Dept. of RTV
Tucson, AZ 85721
Jeff Haskell
602-621-1341

Vintage Recorders
4831 N. 11 St., Ste. D
Phoenix, AZ 85014
Merel Bregante
602-241-0667

Academy of Audio Video Arts
7430 Melrose Ave.
Los Angeles, CA.
Poonam Bali
213-467-5256

Academy of Radio Broadcasting
8907 Warner Ave., #115
Huntington Beach, CA 92647
Tom King
714-842-0100

AEA, Inc.
1029 N. Allen Ave.
Pasadena, CA 91104
Wes Dooley
818-798-9127

Audio Services Corporation
10639 Riverside Dr.
N. Hollywood, CA 91602
Fred Ginsburg
818-980-9891

Bailie School of Broadcast
90 New Montgomery St.
San Francisco, CA 94115
Aldy Swanson
415-541-0707

Blue Bear School of Music
Fort Mason, Bldg. D
San Fracisco, CA 94123
Steve Savage
415-673-3600

California Institute of the Arts
School of Music
24700 McBean Pkwy.
Valencia, CA 91355
Alan Chaplin
805-255-1050

California Prof. Music Business Academy
317 De la Cruz Blvd.
Santa Clara, CA 95050
Hewlett Crist
408-727-3232

California State Polytech University
Music Dept.
San Luis Obispo, CA 93407
Antonio Barata
805-546-2406

California State University-Long Beach
1250 Bellflower Blvd.
Long Beach, CA 90840
Robert Finney
213-498-5404

California State University-Los Angeles
5151 State University Dr.
Los Angeles, CA 90032
Michael Fruchter
213-224-3448

California State University-Chico
Department of Music
Chico, CA 95929
Raymond Barker
916-895-5152

California State University-Fullerton
800 N. State College
Fullerton, CA. 92634
John Fisher
714-773-3442

California State University-Dominguez Hill
Music Department
1000 Victoria St.
Carson, CA 90747
David Champion
213-516-3543

City College of San Francisco
50 Phelan Ave.
San Francisco, CA 94112
Phillip Brown
415-239-3525

CMX Corporation
2230 Martin Ave.
Santa Clara, CA 95050
Susan Dressler
408-988-2000

College for Recording Arts
665 Hamilton St.
San Francisco, CA 94107
Leo De Gar Kulka
415-781-6306

Columbia College
925 N. La Brea Ave.
Los Angeles, CA 90038
William Mayhew
213-851-0550

Foothill College
12345 El Monte Rd.
Los Altos Hills, CA 94022
Richard James
415-948-8590

Fullerton College
Music Dept.
321 E. Chapman Ave.
Fullerton, CA 92634
Alex Cima
714-871-8000

Gavilan Community College
5055 Santa Teresa Blvd.
Gilroy, CA 95020
Art Junker
408-847-1400

Golden West Community College
Dept. of Commercial Music
15744 Golden West Ave.
Huntington Beach, CA 92647
Evan Williams
714-892-7711

Grossmont Community College
8800 Grossmont College Dr.
El Cajon, CA 92020
Elaine McLevie
619-465-1700

Grove School of Music
12754 Venture Blvd.
Studio City, CA 91604
Paul Goldfield
818-904-9400

Institute of Audio/Video Engineering
1831 Hyperion Ave.
Hollywood, CA 90027
Ted Shreffler
800-551-8877

Long Beach City College
4901 Carson St.
Long Beach, CA 90808
George Shaw
213-420-4517

Los Angeles City College
855 N. Vermont Ave.
Los Angeles, CA 90029
J. Robert Stahley
213-669-5545

Los Angeles Harbor College
Music Dept.
1111 Figueroa Pl.
Wilmington, CA 90744
Robert Billings
213-518-1000

Los Angeles Recording Workshop
12268 Ventura Blvd.
Studio City, CA 91604
Chris Knight
818-763-7400

Los Medanos College
2700 E. Leland Rd.
Pittsburgh, CA 94565
Frank Dorritie
415-439-0200

Loyola Marymount University
Dept. of Communications
Los Angeles, CA 90045
Vinay Shrivastava
213-642-3033

Marin Community College
Music Dept.
Kentfield, CA 94904
Tara Flandreau
415-485-9466

Media Sciences Institute
3465 El Cajon Blvd.
San Diego, CA 92104
Richard Bowen
619-280-7454

Mendocino County Office of Education
PO Box 226
Mendocino, CA 95460
Bob Evans
707-937-1200

Mills College
5000 MacArthur Blvd.
Oakland, CA 94613
David Rosenboom
415-430-2191

Miracosta College
One Bernard Dr.
Oceanside, CA 92056
Dave Megill
619-757-2121

Mixmaster Recording Schools
4877 Mercury St.
San Diego, CA 92111
Garth Hedin
619-569-7367

Natural Sound Studio
9851 Prospect Ave.
Sanfee, CA 92071
Jeff Mattazaro
714-448-6000

Recording Engineering Workshop
421 N. Tustin
Orange, CA 92667
Ted Veguari
714-633-8200

Recording Institute
14511 Delano
Los Angeles, CA 91411
Larry Cook
213-254-1756

Saddleback College
28000 Marguerite Pkwy.
Mission Viejo, CA 92692
Greg Bishop
714-582-5727

SAE Los Angeles
3000 S. Robertson
Los Angeles, CA 90034
Cheryl Abott
213-559-0973

San Francisco State University
1600 Holloway Ave.
San Francisco, CA 94132
Mary Pieratt
415-469-1372

San Jose Sate University
Electro Acoustic Studios
1 Washington Square
San Jose, CA 95192
Allen Strange
408-277-2905

Sonoma Sound
PO Box 1623
Sonoma, CA 95476
Arron Johnson
707-996-4363

Sonoma State University
1801 E. Cotati Ave.
Rohnert Park, CA 94928
Warren Dennis
707-664-2324

Sony Broadcast Training Center
677 River Oaks Parkway
San Jose, CA 95134
Mary McGuiness
408-946-9622

Sound Investment Enterprises
PO Box 4139
Thousand Oaks, CA 91359
Jim McCandliss
805-499-0539

Sound Master Schools
10747 Magnolia Blvd.
N. Hollywood, CA 91601
Brian Ingoldsby
213-650-8000

Stanford University
Center for Computer Research in Music &
Acoustics, Dept. of Music
Stanford, CA 94305
John Chowning

Trebas-Los Angeles
6602 Sunset Blvd.
Hollywood, CA 90028
Denise Coyle
213-467-6800

University of Applied Technology
6363 Sunset Blvd., #920
Hollywood, CA 90028
Dr. Wills
213-469-9944

UCLA Extension
10995 Le Conte Ave.
Los Angeles, CA 90024
Helen DeWitty
213-825-9064

University of California-San Diego
Computer Audio Research Lab
Center for Music & Related Research
La Jolla, CA 92093

Univeristy of California-Santa Cruz
133 Communications Bldg.
Santa Cruz, CA 95064
Peter Elsea
408-429-2369

University of California-Riverside
Media Resources Dept.
Riverside, CA 92521
Jerry Gordon
714-787-3041

University of Sound Arts
1645 N. Vine, Ste. 350
Hollywood, CA 90028
Jerry Bernstein
213-467-5256

University of Southern California
School of Music, MUS 102A
University Park, CA 90089
Richard McIlvery
213-743-2627

USA Audio Video
1645 N. Vine St.
Hollywood, CA 90028
Sushie Godwin
213-467-5256

COLORADO

Aim Community College
5401 W. 20th St.
Greeley, CO 80632
George Conger
303-330-8008

Claws-on Productions
1355 "C" Bear MTN Rd.
Boulder, CO 80303
Lisa Clawson
303-499-1144

Denver Public Schools
Career Education Center
2650 Eliot St.
Denver, CO 80211
Joseph Hall
303-455-5966

Media Technology Institute
680 Indiana St.
Golden, CO 80401
Diane Weigle
303-278-2551

University of Colorado-Denver
1100 14th St.
College of Music
Denver, CO 80202
Bill Porter
303-556-2727

CONNECTICUT

Central Connecticut State University
1615 Stanley St.
New Britain, CT 06050
Leroy Temple
203-827-7263

Nickel Recording
168 Buckingham St.
Hartford, CT 06106
Jack Stang
203-524-5656

Northwest Connecticut Community College
Park Pl.
Winsted, CT 06098
Charles Dmytrin
203-379-8543

RBY Recording Studio
920 N. Main St.
Southbury, CT 06488
Marjorie Jones
203-264-3666

Recording Center
25 Van Zant
East Norwalk, CT 06855
Ethan Winer
203-853-3433

Trod Nossel Recording Studios
10 George St., Box 57
Wallingford, CT 06492
Richard Robinson
203-269-4465

University of Hartford
College of Engineering
200 Bloomfield Ave.
West Hartford, CT 06117
Robert Celmer
203-243-4792

University of New Haven
300 Orange Ave.
West Haven, CT 06516
Michael Kaloyanides
203-932-7101

DISTRICT OF COLUMBIA

American University
Dept. of Physics
Washington, DC 20016
Dr. Romeo Segnan
202-686-2548

George Washington University
Music Dept.
Washington, DC 20052
Ulf Grahn
202-994-9037

FLORIDA

Art Institute of Ft. Lauderdale
1799 SE 17th St.
Ft. Lauderdale, FL 33316
John Morn
800-327-7603

Florida State University
Center for Music Research
Tallahassee, FL 32306

Full Sail Center for Recording Arts
658 Douglas Ave.
Altamonte Springs, FL 32714
Jon Phelps
800-221-2747

Josh Noland Music Studio
760 W. Sample Rd.
Pompano Beach, FL 33064
Josh Noland
305-943-9865

Miami Sunset Senior High School
13125 SW 72nd St.
Miami, FL 33183
Daniel Sell
305-385-4255

Sony Professional Audio Training Group
1400 W. Commercial Blvd.
Ft. Lauderdale, FL 33309
David Moore
305-491-0825

Soundshine Productions
723 W. Sunrise Blvd.
Ft. Lauderdale, FL 33311
Paul Avakian
305-463-9882

University of Miami
School of Music
Gusman Hall
Coral Gables, FL 33124
Ken Pohlmann
305-284-2245

GEORGIA

Georgia Institute of Technology
School of Electrical Engineering
Atlanta, GA 30332
W. Marshall Leach
404-894-2963

Georgia State University
Dept. of Commercial Music/Recording
University Plaza
Atlanta, GA 30303
Carter Thomas
404-658-3513

Music Business Institute
2970 Peachtree Rd., NW
Suite 400
Atlanta, GA 30305
Nancy Pomerance
404-231-3303

ILLINOIS

Bradley University
Constance Hall
Peoria, IL 61625
David Vroman
309-677-2595

Columbia College of Chicago
600 S. Michigan Ave.
Chicago, IL 60605
Doug Jones
312-660-1600

Creative Audio
705 Western Ave.
Urbana, IL 61801
Mike Reed
217-367-3530

Elmhurst College
Music Dept.
190 Prospect Ave.
Elmhurst, IL 60126
Tim Hayes
312-279-1400

Hedden West Recorders
1200 Remington Rd.
Schaumburg, IL 60195
Mike Freeman
312-885-1330

Ivs School of Music
722 Lake St.
Oak Park, IL 60301
William Messner
312-848-3008

Millikin University
1184 W. Main
Decatur, IL 62522
Wesley Tower
217-424-6300

Northern Illinois University
School of Music
Dekalb, IL 60115
Thomas Rossing
815-753-6493

Opus Recording Company
4262 Grand Ave.
Gurnee, IL 60031
Tony Pettinato
312-336-6787

Solid Sound Recording Studio
2400 W. Hassell Rd., Ste. 430
Hoffman Estates, IL 60195
Judd Sager
312-882-7446

Sound Trax
1000 W. 7th St.
Bloomington, IL 47401
Joseph Wilson
812-332-7475

Southern Illinois University
Dept. of Cinema & Photography
Carbondale, IL 62901
David Gilmore
618-453-2365

University of Illinois Urbana-Champaign
School of Music
2136 Music Bldg.
Urbana, IL 61801
James Beauchamp
217-333-1089

INDIANA

Anderson College
1100 E. Fifth St.
Anderson, IN 46012
F. Dale Bengtson
317-649-9071

Ball State University
Music Engineering
Muncie, IN 47306
Cleve Scott
317-285-5537

Butler University
Dept. of Radio & Television
4600 Sunset Ave.
Indianapolis, IN 46208
James Phillippe
317-283-9501

Indiana University
School of Music MU 4C
Bloomington, IN 47405
David Pickett
812-335-1900

Purdue University Calumet
Dept. of Electrical Engineering
Hammond, IN 46323
F. David Harris
219-844-0520

Synergetic Audio Concepts
PO Box 1239
Bedford, IN 47421
Don & Carolyn Davis
812-275-3853

Vincennes University
1002 N. 1st St.
Vincennes, IN 47591
Jack Hanes
812-885-4135

IOWA

Iowa State University
Dept. of Engineering
2019 Black Engineering Bldg.
Ames, IA 50011
D.K. Hogler
515-294-7399

University of Iowa
2057 Music Bldg.
Iowa City, IA 52242
Lowell Cross
319-335-1664

KANSAS

Kansas State University
Music Dept.
Manhattan, KS 66502
Hanley Jackson
913-532-5740

St. Mary of the Plains College
San Jose Dr.
Dodge City, KS 67801
Bill Christy
316-225-4171

Sunset Productions
117 W. 8th
Hays, KS 67601
Mark Meckel
913-625-9634

KENTUCKY

Morehead State University
Communications Dept.
Brechinridge Hall
Morehead, KY 40351
Richard Dandeneau
606-783-2134

LOUISIANA

Southeastern Louisiana University
Box 683, SLU
Hammond, LA 70404
Robert Priez
504-549-2334

MAINE

International Film & Television Workshop
Rockport, ME 04859
207-236-8581

University of Maine at Augusta
University Heights
Augusta, ME 04330
Bill Moseley
207-622-7131

MASSACHUSETTS

Audio Workshop School
119 Fresh Pond Parkway
Cambridge, MA 02138
Steve Langstaff
617-547-3957

Berklee College of Music
1140 Boylston St.
Boston, MA 02215
David Moulton
617-266-1400

Bruel & Kjaer Instruments, Inc.
185 Forest St.
Marlborough, MA 01752
Alice McLean
617-481-7000

Emerson College
100 Beacon St.
Boston, MA 02116
617-578-8800

Humphrey Occupational Resources Center
75 New Dudley St.
Boston, MA 02115
Philip Worrell
617-442-5200

Massachusetts Institute of Technology
Acoustics & Vibrations Lab
Dept. of Mechanical Engineering
Cambridge, MA 02139

New England Conservatory of Music
290 Huntington Ave.
Boston, MA 02115
Robert Ceely
617-262-1120

University of Lowell
College of Music
One University Ave.
Lowell, MA 01854
William Moylan
617-452-5000

MARYLAND

JRB Sound Studios
4917 Cordell Ave.
Bethesda, MD 20014
John Burr
301-654-3800

Omega Studios
5609 Fishers Ln.
Rockville, MD 20852
Bob Yesbek
301-230-9100

Peabody Conservatory of Music
1 E. Mt. Vernon Pl.
Baltimore, MD 21218
Alan Kefauver
800-368-2521

Roar Productions
6655-H Dobbin Rd.
Columbia, MD 21045
Andrea Weatherhead
301-596-2600

Slippery Rock University
Music Dept.
Swope Music Bldg.
Slippery Rock, MD 16057
Andrew Glowaty
412-794-7276

MICHIGAN

Henry Ford Community College
5101 Evergreen Rd.
Dearborn, MI 48128
Jay Korinek
313-845-9634

Interlochen Recording Arts Institute
Interlochen Center for the Arts
Interlochen, MI 49643
David Gail
616-276-9221

Lansing Community College
PO Box 40010
Lansing, MI 48901
Lee Thorton
517-483-1673

Michigan State University
409 Communication Arts Bldg.
E. Lansing, MI 48824
Gary Reid
517-355-8372

Michigan Tech University
Dept. of Electrical Engineering
Houghton, MI 49931
Richard Schwartz
906-487-2550

Recording Institute of Detroit
14611 E. 9 Mile Rd.
East Detroit, MI 48021
Robert Dennis
313-779-1380

University of Detroit
3800 Puritan
Detroit, MI 48238
Vivian Dicks
313-927-1173

MINNESOTA

Brown Institute
3123-31 East Lake Rd.
Minneapolis, MN 55406
Bill Johnson
612-721-2481

Hutchinson Vocational Technical Institute
200 Century Ave.
Hutchinson, MN 55350
David Igl
612-587-3636

Inver Hills Community College
8445 E. College Trail
Inver Grove Hgts., MN 55075
Walker Pierce
612-450-8501

Red Wing Technical Institute
AVTI, Highway 58
Red Wing, MN 55066
Chuck Munson
612-388-8271

St. Paul Public Schools
Central Studios
275 N. Lexington
St. Paul, MN 55104
Ben James
612-645-9217

MISSOURI

Chapman Recording Workshop
228 W. 5th
Kansas City, MO 64105
Chuck Chapman
816-842-6854

School of the Ozarks
Jamison Bldg.
Pt. Lookout, MO 65726
Robert Lake
417-334-6411

University of Missouri-Kansas City
Conservatory of Music
4949 Cherry St.
Kansas City, MO 64110
Tom Mardikes
816-276-2964

Webster University
470 E. Lockwood
St. Louis, MO 63119
Art Silverblatt
314-968-7032

MISSISSIPPI

Delta State University
PO Box 3252
Cleveland, MS 38733
601-846-4610

MONTANA

May School of Broadcasting & Technology
PO Box 127
Billings, MT 59103
Mike May
406-248-4888

NEBRASKA

Northeast Community College
801 E. Benjamin Ave.
Norfolk, NE 68701
Tim Miller
402-644-0506

NEW HAMPSHIRE

Dartmouth College
Dean of Graduate Studies
School of Music
Hanover, NH 03755
Jon Appleton
603-646-3960

NEW JERSEY

Brookdale Community College
Newman Springs Rd.
Lincroft, NJ 07738
Louis Pullano
201-842-1900

Eastern Artist Recording Studio
36 Meadow St.
East Orange, NJ 07017
Howard Kessler
201-673-5680

Jersey City State College
2039 Kennedy Blvd.
Jersey City, NJ 07305
Richard Scott
201-547-3151

Middlesex County College
Woodbridge Ave.
Edison, NJ 08817
Jack Weintraub

Pyramid Recording
331 W. Palisade Ave.
Englewood, NJ 07631
Louis Massa
201-569-7327

NEW MEXICO

Quincy Street Workshop
130 Quincy St. NE
Albuquerque, NM 87108
Eric Larson
505-265-5689

NEW YORK

Aspen Audio Recording Institute
250 W. 54th St.
10th Floor East
New York, NY 10019
Dan Craik
212-581-2196

Audio Recording Technology Institute
756 Main St.
Farmingdale, NY 11735
Jim Bernard
516-454-8999

Cayuga Community College
Telecommunications Dept.
Franklin St.
Auburn, NY 13021
315-255-1743

Center for Electronic Music
432 Park Ave. South
New York, NY 10016
Howard Massey
212-686-1755

Center for Media Arts
226 W. 26th St.
New York, NY 10001
Harry Hirsch
212-807-6670

College of St. Rose
Music Division
432 Western Ave.
Albany, NY 12203
Robert Sheehan
518-454-5178

Community College of the Finger
Lakes
Lincoln Hill
Canandaigua, NY 14424
Frank Verget
716-394-3500

Digital Music Center
155 W. 46th St.
New York, NY 10036
Steve Friedman
212-302-4606

Dutchess Community College
Pendell Rd.
Poughkeepsie, NY 12601
Rich Woods
914-471-4500

Eastman School of Music
26 Gibbs St.
Rochester, NY 14604
David Peelle
716-275-3180

Five Towns College
2165 Seaford Ave.
Seaford, NY 11783
Stanley Cohen
516-783-8800

Houghton College
School of Music
Houghton, NY 14744
Robert Galoway
716-567-2211

Institute Hispano de Audio
130 W. 42nd St., Rm 551
New York, NY 10036
Jose Gallegos
212-221-6625

Institute of Audio Research
64 University Pl.
Greenwich Village
New York, NY 10003
Philip Stein
212-677-7580

Musication
1600 Broadway, Ste. 1000A
New York, NY 10019
J. Blackman
212-957-9101

New School
Media Studies Program
2 W. 13th St.
New York, NY 10011
Peter Haratonik
212-741-8903

New York University
Music Education
35 W. 4th St., Rm 777
New York, NY 10003
David Sanders
212-998-5424

Recording Institute of America
45 W. 57th, 7th Flr.
New York, NY 10019
212-753-6447

Rochester Institute of Technology
Electrical Engineering Dept.
Rochester, NY 14623
W.F. Walker
716-475-2174

Ross Creative Music
51 Barton Pl.
Port Chester, NY 10573
Mark Ross
914-939-0317

Select Sound Recording Studio
2315 Elmwood Ave.
Kenmore, NY 14217
Chuck Mandrell
716-873-2717

Skidmore College
Music Dept.
Saratoga Springs, NY 12866
Charles Joseph
518-584-5000

SUNY Fredonia
School of Music
Mason Hall
Fredonia, NY 14063
John Maier
716-673-3151

SUNY Oneonta
115 Fine Arts Center
Oneonta, NY 13820
John Mazarak
607-431-3415

SUNY Plattsburgh
103 Yokum Hall
Plattsburgh, NY 12901
Jerry Supple
518-564-2111

Syracuse University
Newhouse School
215 University Place
Syracuse, NY 13244
Ernest Martin
315-423-4004

Turning Mill Inc.
PO Box L
Palenville, NY 12463
Lucy Swenson
518-678-9293

NEVADA

CSS Recording Studio
2010 E. Charleston Blvd.
Las Vegas, NV 89104
Debbie Parks
702-384-1212

University of Nevada- Las Vegas
4505 S. Maryland Pkwy.
Las Vegas, NV 89154
Curt Miller
702-739-0819

NORTH CAROLINA

North Carolina State University
Center for Sound & Vibration
Campus Box 7910
Raleigh, NC 27695

University of North Carolina- Asheville
Music Dept.
Lipinsky Hall
Asheville, NC 28804
Wayne Kirby
704-251-6432

Weaver Education Center
300 S. Spring St.
Greensboro, NC 27401
Howard Braxton
919-370-8282

Western Carolina University
Radio Dept.
Cullowhee, NC 28723
Don Loeffler
704-227-7491

William G. Enloe High School
128 Clarendon Crescent
Raleigh, NC 27610
Diane Payne
919-755-6660

OHIO

Beachwood Studios
23330 Commerce Park
Beachwood, OH 44122
George Sipl
216-292-7300

Bowling Green State University
College of Music Arts
Bowling Green, OH 43403
Mark Bunce
419-372-8405

Capital University
Conservatory of Music
2119 E. Main St.
Columbus, OH 43209
Robert Breihaupt
614-236-6574

Case Western Reserve University
Center for Music & Technology
Dept. of Music, Haydn Hall
Cleveland, OH 44106

Cleveland Institute of Music
11021 East Blvd.
Cleveland, OH 44106
Tom Knab
216-791-5165

Lakeland Community College
State Routes 306 & I-90
Mentor, OH 44060
Charles Frank
216-953-7000

Oberlin College
Conservatory of Music
Oberlin, OH 44074
Conrad Cummings
216-773-8200

Ohio State University
Music Dept.
1866 College Rd.
Columbus, OH 43210
Robert Lackey
614-422-7899

Recording Workshop
455-X Massieville Rd.
Chillicothe, OH 45601
Jim Rosebrook
800-848-9900

Southern Ohio College
1055 Laidlaw Ave.
Cincinnati, OH 45237
Mark Turner
513-242-3791

<u>*OKLAHOMA*</u>

Cameron University
2800 W. Gore
Lawton, OK 73505
Mark Norman
405-581-2425

Oklahoma State University
Center for the Performing Arts
Stillwater, OK 74078
Gerald Frank
405-624-6133

Rose State College
6420 SE 15th
Midwest City, OK 73110
Larry Nutter
405-733-7426

University of Oklahoma
860 Van Vleet Oval
Norman, OK 73069
Elizabeth Yamashita
405-325-2721

<u>*OREGON*</u>

Portland Community College
12000 SW 49th Ave.
Music Dept.
Portland, OR 97219
Hal Lee
503-283-2541

Recording Associates
5821 SE Powell Blvd.
Portland, OR 97206
Jay Webster
503-777-4621

<u>*PENNSYLVANIA*</u>

Bucks County Community College
Media & Performing Arts Dept.
Newton, PA 18940
William Brenner
215-968-8085

Duquesne University
Television Studio
509 DPCC
Pittsburgh, PA 15282
Melanie Dudash
412-434-6090

Evergreen Recording Arts Seminars
1373 McLaughlin Run Rd.
Pittsburgh, PA 15241
Thomas Kikta
412-221-2737

Iris Sound Studio
237 Main St.
Royersford, PA 19468
David Ivory
215-948-3448

Jon Miller School of Recording Arts
2524 E. Scenic Dr.
Bath, PA 18014
Jon Miller

JTM Workshop of Recording Arts
Best Ave., Box 686
Knox, PA 16232
Frank Battista
814-797-5883

Lebanon Valley College
Music Dept.
College Ave.
Annville, PA 17003
John Uhl
717-867-4411

Pennsylvania State University
Graduate Acoustics Program
Applied Science Bldg., Box 30
State College, PA 16804
Jiri Tichy
814-865-6364

Pennsylvania State University
Sound & Recording Workshops
220 Special Services Bldg.
University Park, PA 16802
Peter Kiefer
814-863-2911

Starr Recording Studio
210 Saint James Pl.
Philadelphia, PA 19106
Rose Payne
215-925-5265

University of Pennsylvania
School of Electrical Engineering
Philadelphia, PA 19104
O.M.Salati

York College of Pennsylvania
Coutry Club Road
York, PA 17403
Thomas Hall
717-846-7788

PUERTO RICO

International American University of PR
P.O.Box 1293
Hato Rey, PR 00919
Sylvia Rodriguez
809-758-8000

SOUTH CAROLINA

Bob Jones University
1700 Wade Hamton Blvd.
Greenville, SC 29614
Dwight Gustafson
803-242-5100

Converse College
School of Music
Spartanburg, SC 29301
Henry Janiec
803-596-9021

Strawberry Jam Recording Studio
3964 Apian Way
W. Columbia, SC 29164
Mary Curlee
803-356-4540

TENNESSEE

American Institute of Technology
1101 Kermit Dr., Ste. LL-5
Nashville, TN 37217
Ed Sheppard
615-360-3300

Davidson Technical College
212 Pavilion Blvd.
Nashville, TN 37217
Suzanne Davidson
615-360-3300

Franklin Institute of Recording Sound Tech.
PO Box 1121
Franklin, TN 37065
615-794-3660

Memphis State University
Commercial Music Program
Dept. of Music
Memphis, TN 38152
Larry Lipman
901-454-2559

Middle Tennessee State University
PO Box 21 - MTSU
Murfreesboro, TN 37132
Geoffrey Hull
615-898-2813

University of Tennessee
Music Dept.
1741 Volunteer Blvd.
Knoxville, TN 37996
Kenneth Jacobs
615-974-5486

TEXAS

Abilene Christine University
1600 Campus Ct.
Abilene, TX 79699
Larry Bradshaw
915-674-2311

Alvin Community College
3110 Mustang Road
Alvin, TX 77511
Cathy Forsythe
713-331-6111

Art Institute of Dallas
Two Northpark
8080 Parklane
Dallas, TX 75231
Lee Colker
800-441-8086

Cedar Valley Community College
3030 N. Dallas Ave.
Lancaster, TX 75134
Dr. Davidson
214-372-8120

East Texas State University
Music Dept.
ET Station
Commerce, TX 75428
Ronald Yates
214-886-5303

Frank Phillips College
PO Box 5118
Borger, TX 79008
Bob Ramsey
806-274-5311

Goodnight Dallas Recording School
11260 Goodnight Ln.
Dallas, TX 75229
Ruben Ayala
214-241-5182

Houston Community College
901 Yorkshester
Houston, TX 77079
Aubrey Tucker
713-468-6891

Klarr Broadcasting Network
PO Box 3842
Houston, TX 77253
Lawrence Herbst

Lincoln Institute
7622 Louette Rd.
Spring, TX 77379
J.E. Lincoln
713-376-9679

McClennan Community College
1400 College Dr.
Waco, TX 76708
David Hibbard
817-756-6551

Midland College
3600 N. Garfield
Midland, TX 79705
Gerald Tubb
915-685-4648

North Texas State University
Box 5128
Denton, TX 76203
Donald Staples

Pharr-San Juan-Alamo High School
1229 S. "I" Rd.
Pharr, TX 78577
Adam Farias
512-787-4289

San Antonio College
RTF Dept.
1300 San Pdro
San Antonio, TX 78284
Fred Weiss
512-733-2793

Skip Frazee Audio Engineering School
3341 Towerwood, Ste. 206
Dallas, TX 75234
Skip Frazee
214-243-3735

Sound Arts Recording Studios
2036 Pasket, Ste. A
Houston, TX 77092
Barbara Pennington
713-688-8067

South Plaines College
1400 College Ave.
Levelland, TX 79336
Randy Ellis
806-894-9611

Tarrant County Junior College
828 Harwood Rd.
Hurst, TX 76054
Herman Crow
817-281-7860

Temple Junior College
2600 S. 1st St.
Tempe, TX 76504
Bill Christy
817-773-9961

Texarkana College
Recording Studios
2500 N. Robison Rd.
Texarkana, TX 75501
Murray Alewine
214-838-4541

Texas Christian University
PO Box 30793
Ft. Worth, TX 76129
Terry Ellmore
817-921-7630

Texas Tech University
Box 4710
Dept. of Mass Communications
Lubbock, TX 79409
Dennis Harp
806-742-3382

Trinity University
715 Stadium Dr.
San Antonio, TX 78284
Robert Blanchard
512-736-8113

University of North Texas
Division of RTVF
Box 13108
Denton, TX 76203
John Kuiper
817-565-2537

UTAH

Audio Recording Arts Academy
PO Box 8398
Salt Lake City, UT 84108
Tracy Jorgensen
801-581-1400

Brigham Young University
Dept. of Music
C-550 Harris Fine Arts Center
Provo, UT 84602
James Anglesey
801-378-3083

VERMONT

University of Vermont
Communications Dept.
Burlington, VT 05401
Brian Marshall
802-656-3214

VIRGINIA

Alpha Studio
2049 W. Broad St.
Richmond, VA 23220
Eric Johnson
804-358-3952

Hampton University
Dept. of Music
Recording Studio
Hampton, VA 23666
Bob Ransom
804-727-5514

Tidewater Community College
1700 College Crescent
Virginia Beach, VA 23456
Sam Ebersole
804-427-7294

WASHINGTON

Battle Ground High School
204 W. Main
Battle Ground, WA 98604
Stephen Cox
206-687-5171

Cornish College of Arts
710 Roy St.
Seattle, WA 98102
Jane Lambert
206-323-1400

Crow Recording Studios
4000 Wallington Ave. N.
Seattle, WA 98103
Tod Crooks
206-634-3088

Eastern Washington University
Dept. of Radio & Television
Cheney, WA 99004
Ray Barnes
509-359-2228

Evergreen College
LIB 1326 TESC
Olympia, WA 98505
Peter Randlette
206-866-6000

Horizon Recording Studio
1317 S. 295th Pl.
Federal Way, WA 98003
Bill Gibson
206-941-2018

Kearney Barton's Audio Recording School
4718 38th Ave., NE
Seattle, WA 98105
Kearney Barton
206-525-7372

Pacific Lutheran University
121st & Park Ave.
Tacoma, WA 98447
Bob Holden
206-535-7268

WISCONSIN

Career Institute of Audio Engineering
PO Box 396
Kenosha, WI 53141
Jeff Harmon
414-656-0717

Kennedy Recording Studios
8006 W. Appleton Ave.
Milwaukee, WI 53218
David Kennedy
414-273-5720

Marquette University
Computer Speech Processing Research Lab
1515 W. Wisconsin Ave.
Milwaukee, WI 53233

Trans America School of Broadcasting
108 Scott St.
Wausau, WI 54401
Chris Hutchings
715-842-1000

University of Wisconsin- Madison
Dept. of Electrical Engineering
1415 Johnson Dr.
Madison, WI 53706
R.A. Greiner
608-262-9655

University of Wisconsin- Oshkosh
800 Algoma Blvd.
Oshkosh, WI 54901
Charles Isaacson
414-424-4224

University of Wisconsin- La Crosse
Educational Media
La Crosse, WI 54601
D. Wick
608-785-8649

WYOMING

Casper College
125 College Dr.
Casper, WY 82601
Terry Gundersen
307-268-2532

Foreign Schools

AUSTRALIA

Queensland Conservatorium of Music
Dept. of Music Technology
PO Box 28
North Quay, QLD 4000
AUSTRALIA
Dan Fournier
617-229-2650

Royal Melbourne Institute of Technology
80 Victoria St.
Carlton, Victoria 3053
AUSTRALIA
Rodney Staples
03-663-5611

S.A. Music & Audio Education Centre
212 Hindley St.
Adelaide 5000
AUSTRALIA
Peter Brook
08-212-5955

SAE Adelaide
263 North Tce.
Adelaide SA
AUSTRALIA
08-223-3535

SAE Brisbane
22 Heussler Tce.
Milton QLD 4064
Brisbane
AUSTRALIA
07-369-8108

SAE Melbourne
80-86 Inkerman St.
St. Kilda VIC 3182
AUSTRALIA
09-994-4409

SAE Perth
42 Wickham St.
East Perth WA
AUSTRALIA
09-325-4533

SAE Sydney
68-72 Wentworth Ave.
Sydney NSW 2010
AUSTRALIA
T. Misner
02-211-3711

Victoria Audio Education Centre
1-3 Gordon St.
Richmond, Victoria 3121
AUSTRALIA
Vyt Karazija
03-428-1190

AUSTRIA

SAE Vienna
Mayerhofgasse 4
Vienna A-1040
AUSTRIA
A. Gall
222-65-27-18

Universite Graz
Inffeldgasse 12
A-8010 Graz
AUSTRIA

BELGIUM

INSAS
8 Rue Theresienne
B-1000 Brussels
BELGIUM

Institut des Arts de Diffusion
38-40 Rue des Blancs-Chevaux
B-1348 Louvain la Neuve
BELGIUM

National Radio en Film Institut
Victor Rousseaulaan 75
B-1110 Brussels
BELGIUM

CANADA

Banff Centre School of Fine Arts
Box 1020
Banff, Alberta
CANADA T0L 0C0
George Ross
403-762-6100

Bullfrog Recording School
2475 Dunbar St.
Vancouver, BC
CANADA V6R 3N2
Maggie Scherf
604-734-4617

Camtek Audio Productions, Inc.
15112-116 A Ave.
Edmonton, Alberta
CANADA
Sandi Guse
403-452-6910

Columbia Academy of Recording
1295 W. Broadway
Vancouver, BC
CANADA V6H 3X8
George McNeill
604-736-3316

George Brown College of Arts & Technology
PO Box 1015
Station B
Toronto, Ontario
CANADA
Roger Starker
416-967-1212

Institute of Communication Arts
12-12840 Bathgate Way
Richmond, BC
V6V 1Z4 CANADA
Niels Hartvig-Nielsen
604-278-0232

McGill University
Music Dept.
555 Sherbrooke St. W.
Montreal, Quebec
CANADA H3A 1E3
Wieslaw Woszcyk
514-392-4546

Ontario Institute of Audio Recording Technology
500 Newbold St.
London, Ontario
N6E 1K6 CANADA
Geoff Keymer
519-686-5010

Recording Arts Program of Canada
28 Valrose Dr.
Stoney Creek, Ontario
CANADA L8E 3T4
Nick Keca
416-662-2666

Trebas-Montreal
1435 Bleury, #301
Montreal, Quebec
CANADA H3A 2H7
Jacques Michaud
514-845-4141

Trebas-Ottawa
290 Nepean St.
Ottawa, Ontario
CANADA K1R 5G3
James Henderson
613-232-7104

Trebas-Toronto
410 Dundas St. E.
Toronto, Ontario
CANADA M5A 2A8
Kerry Keeler
416-966-3066

Trebas-Vancouver
112 E. 3rd Ave.
Vancouver, BC
CANADA V5T 1C8
Anne Arthur
604-872-2666

University of Waterloo
Audio Research Group
Waterloo, Ontario
CANADA N2L 3G1
Stanley Lipshitz
519-885-1211

Universal Institute of Recording Arts
2190 W. 12th Ave.
Vancouver, BC
CANADA V6K 2N2
Robert Leong
604-734-2922

DENMARK

Aalborg University
Institute of Electronic Systems
Fredrik Bajers Vej 7
DK-9220 Aalborg 0
DENMARK
Henrik Moller
45-8-154811

Danish Acoustical Institute
Gregersensvej 3
DK-2630 Taastrup
DENMARK
Jan Vostmann
02-99-77-55

FRANCE

Ecole Superieure de Realisation Audio
135 Avenue Felix Faure
Paris 75015
FRANCE
Robert Caplain
1-454-5658

ITALY

EMIT
Piazza Cantore 10
I-20123 Milan
ITALY
02-83-23-290

JAPAN

Kyusha Institute of Design
Waseda, 262 Shiobara
Minami Fukuoka, 815
JAPAN
092-541-1431

NETHERLANDS

Koninklyk Conservatorium
Juliana van Stolberglaan 1
2595 CA's - Gravenhage
NETHERLANDS
Peter Nuyten
070-814251

SAE Utrecht
Voorstaat 9
3512 AH -Utrecht
NETHERLANDS
030-321-060

NORWAY

Norsk Lydskole
Christian Kroghsgate 2
N-0186 Oslo
NORWAY

POLAND

Chopin's Academy of Music
Sound Recording Facility
M. Okolnik 2
Warsaw, POLAND

UNITED KINGDOM

Assoc. of Professional Recording Schools
163 A High St.
Rickmansworth WD 3 1AY
UNITED KINGDOM

Gateway School of Recording & Music Tech
Kingston Hill Centre
School of Music
Surrey KT2 7LB
UNITED KINGDOM
01-549-0014

London College of Furniture
Music Instrument Technology
41 Commercial Rd.
London E1 1LA
UNITED KINGDOM
Tim Orr
01-247-1953

Media Production Services
Bon Marche Bldg.
Ferndale Rd.
London SW9 8EJ
UNITED KINGDOM
01-274-4000

SAE London
St. Marks Bldg.
Chillingworth Rd.
London N7 8JQ
UNITED KINGDOM
S. Quinn
01-609-2653

SAE Manchester
Beehive Mills, 5th Flr.
Manchester M1
UNITED KINGDOM

Thames Television Limited
Teddington Studios
Teddington, Middlesex TW11 9NT
UNITED KINGDOM
Karen McLaren
01-977-3252

University of Surrey
Dept. of Music
Guilford, Surrey GU2 5XH
UNITED KINGDOM
David Pickett

WEST GERMANY

Detmold Tonmeister Institut
Allee 2
D-4930 Detmold
WEST GERMANY
Werner Czesla
5231-26945

Fachhochschule Dusseldorf
Fachberich Electrotechnik
Josef Gockelnstrasse 9
4 Dusseldorf Nord
WEST GERMANY
434715-18

Hochschule der Kunste Berlin
Fasanenstrasse 1-3
Berlin 12
D1000
WEST GERMANY
Prof. Feldgen
030-31850

Institute of Electroacoustics
Technical University Munchen
Munchen D8000
WEST GERMANY
Hugo Fastl
089-21058541

SAE Berlin
Seestrasse 64
Berlin 61
WEST GERMANY
Tom Misner

SAE Frankfurt
Taunus Strasse 44
Frankfurt 1
WEST GERMANY
069-23-61-79

SAE Munich
Weissenburger Strasse 19
8000 Munich 80
WEST GERMANY
A. Forsthofer
089-48-71-45

Bibliography

Audio Engineering Society Directory of Educational Programs, 1980-1988, AES Educational Committee

Directory of Recording Schools, Seminars and Programs 1985, 1986, 1987, 1988, Mix, July 1985-1988

Dunn, Karen. School Studios: Budget or Bust, Mix, July 1988, p. 57

Eargle, John. SPARS On-line: Making It To The Top, Recording Engineer/Producer, June 1988, p. 14

Fay, Michael. Think...Audio, Recording Engineer/Producer, April 1988, p. 4

Fay, Michael. So You Want To Be An Engineer, Recording Engineer/Producer, February 1988, p. 4

Gressel, Josh. Recording School Education Today: Both Roots and Wings, Mix, July 1987, p. 77-80

Helmers, Gary. SPARS On-line, Recording Engineer/Producer, August 1987, p.22

Helmers, Gary. SPARS On-line, Recording Engineer/Producer, June 1987, p. 22

Igl, David. Student Participation: Good Ideas, Excellent Learning, Mix, July 1988, p. 62

Jackson, Blair. Reel Careers. Mix, July 1986, p. 52-58

Jacobson, Linda. Educators Talk About Recording Schools, Mix, July 1985, p. 58-65

Jacobson, Linda. Studios Speak to the Schools, Mix, July 1988, p. 70

Lambert, Mel. RE/P 1987 Salary Survey, Recording Engineer Producer, June 1987, p. 24-39

Moylan, William. Employment Trends, Recording Engineer/Producer, December 1988, p. 30-38

Pohlmann, Ken. Audio Applications: Education Strategies, Mix, July 1985, p. 15-18

Polon, Martin. Perspective: Future for the Aspiring Audio Professional, Studio Sound, February 1988, p. 54-56

Poyten, Paul. The Manufacturer's Role in Education, Mix, July 1988, p. 61

Pro Sound News. 1988 Recording Studio Operations Survey, Pro Sound News, August 1988, p. 35-38

Soifer, Rosanne. On the Job Training-An Overview, Recording Engineer/Producer, January 1988, p. 6

Spencer-Allen, Keith. Where Will the Industries Future Experts Come From?, Studio Sound, March 1988, p. 5

Stone, Chris. SPARS On-line: Making Good Money in the Audio Business, Recording Engineer/Producer, November 1988, p. 16-18

Torchia, Dan. RE/P Second Annual Salary Survey, Recording Engineer/Producer, November 1988, p. 42-56

Suggested Readings on the Past, Present, and Future

Brand, Stewart. The Media Lab: Inventing the Future at M.I.T., New York: Viking Penquin Inc., 1988
The Media Lab investigates the cutting edge of academic research and development in converging electronic media.

Camras, Marvin. Magnetic Recording Handbook, New York: Van Nostrand Reinhold Co., Inc. 1988
Camras' new book is a comprehensive study of magnetic recording history, development, and application of various formats.

Faulkner, Robert. Music on Demand: Composers and Careers in the Hollywood Film Industry, New Brunswick: Transaction Books, 1983
This is an interesting look at the realities of the film and television music composition industry. Music on Demand exposes the social aspects of the business.

Faulkner, Robert. Hollywood Studio Musicians: Their Work and Careers in the Recording Industry, Lanham: University Press of America, 1985
Originally published in 1971, this study is based on research from 1965 to 1968, and provides an interesting historical perspective on the studio musician's role in the industry.

Malm, Krister and Wallis Roger. Big Sounds From Small Peoples: The Music Industry in Small Countries, London: Constable and Co., Ltd., 1984
Based on the findings of the Music in Small Countries project, Big Sounds From Small Peoples details the impact of the recording business on 12 diverse countries' music and culture. An excellent study of dynamic interaction.

Read, Oliver and Welch, Walter. From Tinfoil to Stereo: Evolution of the Phonograph, Indianapolis: Howard W. Sams, 1976
Tracing the development of the phonograph, From Tinfoil to Stereo provides insight into the relationship between the elements that shape and influence emerging audio technologies.